FROM THE PAGES OF
QOHELETH
AN ILLUSTRATED COMMENTARY OF ECCLESIASTES

DR. STEVEN A. JIRGAL

Published by The Core Media Group, Inc., P.O. Box 2037, Indian Trail, NC 28079.

Printed in the United States of America.

To my long-time friend, mentor, and brother in the Lord, Reverend Stephen M. Crotts, an example of wisdom on two feet.

TABLE OF CONTENTS

INTRODUCTION

There can be no better place to be than at the feet of Jesus. There we find the will of God for living under the hand of God as well as the means for living in the presence of God. Secondarily to that scenario might very well be sitting at the feet of King Solomon. There we find the perspective to live in this life with thoughts of, and preparation for the next life.

As we dive into this illustrated commentary on the writings of Solomon, it is very important that we try to grasp what he is saying in a wholistic manner. To grasp only one or two of his statements might very well lead us to despair. But if we step back and try to inculcate the full orb of what he is saying, we'll gain a great perspective on living with others under the pleasure of God.

It is similar to the way one would look at a fine piece of artwork. If one stands a few inches from any painting, he may notice some of the colors, but he will miss the painting in its entirety. But by standing back a few paces, one can grasp the entire picture, enjoy its beauty and appreciate the work of excellence.

With this thought in mind, I invite you and encourage you to stand back from the individual statements of Solomon and grasp the beauty of his writing.

In Proverbs. 22: 17-21, Solomon seems to be begging those who will listen when he says,

> *17Incline your ear and hear the words of the wise,*
> *And apply your mind to my knowledge;*
> *18 For it will be pleasant if you keep them within you,*

That they may be ready on your lips.
[19] So that your trust may be in the Lord,
I have taught you today, even you.
[20] Have I not written to you excellent things
Of counsels and knowledge,
[21] To make you know the certainty of the words of truth
That you may correctly answer him who sent you?

In short, Solomon is saying sternly to his audience, "Listen up!" It is with that attitude that we enter into a closer look at the words of King Solomon in the book of Ecclesiastes.

Ecclesiastes is one of five books classified as *wisdom literature*. Among these are: Job, Psalms, Proverbs, Ecclesiastes, and the Song of Solomon. While speaking with a friend (Rev. Stephen Crotts) he shared with me that he likened the wisdom literature to a college student going from one level of learning to another. Each book served as a prerequisite for the next course.

Proverbs is Life 101. In it you find that life carries with it certain tendencies (not guarantees). If you act a certain way life tends to respond appropriately. The equation for this might be A+B=C.

The book of Job could be compared to Life 201. Job and his friends are under the misconception that good things happen to righteous people and bad things happen to unrighteous people. They held that God blesses those who bless Him with their lives, and He curses those who curse Him with their lives. However, what we find in the life of Job is the formula: A+B does not *always* =C.

In Ecclesiastes we come to Life 301. We learn that although the pieces don't always make sense, the process and episodes of life still carry significance and warrant our attention. Here we learn that A+B may not =C, but A matters, B matters and C matters.

In the book of Psalms we are enrolled in Life 401. Here we find the worship of God through poetry and song. Here is where one learns to lift up the name of the Lord of A, B, and C.

In graduate school the Song of Solomon is our text. In it the lessons of courting, bonding, intimacy, encouragement, disagreement, and redemption are seen. Here is where a mature student learns that God has not given marriage to make us happy, but that it is intended to make us holy. Unconditional love and commitment, along with sacrifice and service are to be the key themes in the lives of those who are married. Here we see demonstrated that A+B may not always equal C, but there is sweetness and mysteries in life.

During the canonization process of the Old Testament, there were three books in danger of exclusion. The book of Esther was questioned due to the fact that the name of God is never mentioned.

The Song of Solomon was on the list due to its steamy themes and sexual references. In fact, in early Hebrew culture, a young man was forbidden to read the book until he reached the age of seventeen.

The book of Ecclesiastes (a person who calls an assembly) was questioned due to the nature of the book. On the surface it seems highly pessimistic. Vanity or futility is woven throughout the entire writing. In fact, it its twelve chapters the word "Vanity" is used no less than sixteen times. (New American Standard Bible)

Yet this book is ripe with wisdom dished out in short pithy points that if reflected on properly can be of great benefit to the reader. Studying it with the goal of gleaning wisdom can propel a person into a position of knowledge that will hold them in good stead throughout life.

Still, preaching from the book of Ecclesiastes is rare except for small references to support a particular point. Seldom do you hear of a preacher preaching through the entire book, and commentaries on it are not as easy to find as they are for other books.

Sounding the depths of Ecclesiastes is avoided due to four main reasons:

1. It is not comfortable acknowledging that life is not under our control.

2. We don't like the idea that total knowledge is impossible to have. In fact, it seems like the more we know, the less we understand. It seems that before long we will know everything and understand nothing.

3. We are not pleased with the possibility that our life will not have any lasting impact. We will live for a certain amount of time, exchange carbon dioxide for oxygen, breath our last,

and then be placed in the ground. No one wants to hear that!

4. The directives and advice are scattered. We like instructions that are neat, clean, and organized. Ecclesiastes seems to jump back and forth among themes and commands. When you are headed in one direction, it seems to shift to another emphasis. This makes it hard to develop continuity.

Not all scholars agree on the authorship of the book. But great evidence is given suggesting Solomon as the writer. He calls himself the *Son of David, King in Jerusalem*. Solomon was the only son of David to rule over Israel from Jerusalem. Both Jewish and Christian tradition hold him as the author. It is on this assumption that we will move throughout the book.

Some have said that the order of the three books written by Solomon reflect different ages and stages he was in while writing. The Song of Solomon was written when he was young and energetic. Proverbs was developed when he had gotten some age, experience and wisdom under his belt. Ecclesiastes was penned when Solomon had tasted all life had to offer and was looking back on the futility of so much of his life. It's this raw view of life that makes the book so valuable. Pain, suffering, disappointment, and despair run rampant throughout the book with the conclusion that ultimately, God is in charge and we are not. He is the source of our hope and encouragement. Life is made better by Him and not by our own efforts.

It is important to look into the background of Solomon to gain a glimpse of his wisdom and perhaps visit his mindset as he went about his pursuit of experience and adventure.

In 1 Kings 3:6-13, we are exposed to the headwaters of the wisdom of King Solomon. He was in Gibeon when the Lord appeared to him in a dream and asked him what he desired from God.

> *[6]Then Solomon said, "You have shown great lovingkindness to Your servant David my father, according as he walked before You in truth and righteousness and uprightness of heart toward You; and You have reserved for him this great lovingkindness, that You have given him a son to sit on his throne, as it is this day. [7] Now, O Lord*

my God, You have made Your servant king in place of my father David, yet I am but a little child; I do not know how to go out or come in. ⁸ Your servant is in the midst of Your people which You have chosen, a great people who are too many to be numbered or counted. ⁹ So give Your servant an understanding heart to judge Your people to discern between good and evil. For who is able to judge this great people of Yours?"

¹⁰It was pleasing in the sight of the Lord that Solomon had asked this thing. ¹¹ God said to him, "Because you have asked this thing and have not asked for yourself long life, nor have asked riches for yourself, nor have you asked for the life of your enemies, but have asked for yourself discernment to understand justice, ¹² behold, I have done according to your words. Behold, I have given you a wise and discerning heart, so that there has been no one like you before you, nor shall one like you arise after you. ¹³ I have also given you what you have not asked, both riches and honor, so that there will not be any among the kings like you all your days.

Some distinctions must be made in viewing this special encounter Solomon had with God:

- He recognized how good God had been to his father David.
- He understands that his kingship was due to the kindness of the Lord.
- He realized that he was not equipped to lead such a great people.
- He acknowledged his need of the hand of God to guide him with such a heavy responsibility.

So, the King asks God for understanding and discernment in order to lead the people of God.

God replies that because Solomon did not ask for what most men would request-such as long life, riches, revenge on his enemies, He was going to give him a wise and discerning heart. In fact, God promised to give him wisdom and discernment beyond those

who came before him and unmatched by anyone who would follow him. God also promised him riches and honor exceeding all his
contemporaries.

We recognize the vast wisdom of King Solomon even today. This
is demonstrated when our attention is drawn to a person who displays great wisdom or depth of understanding. We label their mental abilities as *Solomonic Wisdom*.

Solomon who reigned in Jerusalem for forty years (970-931 B.C.),
amassed tremendous wealth in accordance to the Lord's promise. 2
Chronicles 9 gives us a glimpse of his massive wealth:

> [13] *"Now the weight of gold which came to Solomon in
> one year was 666 talents of gold, [14]besides that which
> the traders and merchants brought; and all the kings of
> Arabia and the governors of the country brought gold
> and silver to Solomon. [15] King Solomon made 200 large
> shields of beaten gold, using 600 shekels of beaten gold
> on each large shield. [16] He made300 shields of beaten
> gold using three hundred shekels of gold on each shield,
> and the king put them in the house of the forest of Leba-
> non.*
>
> [17] *Moreover, the king made a great throne of ivory and
> overlaid it with pure gold. [18] There were six steps to the
> throne and a footstool in gold attached to the throne,
> and arms on each side of the seat, and two lions stand-
> ing beside the arms. [19] Twelve lions were standing there
> on the six steps on the one side and on the other; noth-
> ing like it was made for any other kingdom. [20] All King
> Solomon's drinking vessels were of gold, and all the ves-
> sels of the house of the forest of Lebanon were of pure
> gold; silver was not considered valuable in the days of
> Solomon. [21] For the king had ships which went to Tarshish
> with the servants of Huram; once every three years the
> ships of Tarshish came bringing gold and silver, ivory and
> apes and peacocks.*
>
> [22] *So King Solomon became greater than all the kings
> of the earth in riches and wisdom. [23] And all the kings
> of the earth were seeking the presence of Solomon, to*

hear his wisdom which God had put in his heart. ^{24} They brought every man his gift, articles of silver and gold, garments, weapons, spices, horses and mules, so much year by year.

^{25} Now Solomon had 4,000 stalls for horses and chariots and 12,000 horsemen, and he stationed them in the chariot cities and with the king in Jerusalem. ^{26} He was the ruler over all the kings from the Euphrates River even to the land of the Philistines, and as far as the border of Egypt. ^{27} The king made silver as common as stones in Jerusalem, and he made cedars as plentiful as sycamore trees that are in the lowland. ^{28} And they were bringing horses for Solomon from Egypt and from all countries.

With these thoughts in mind, the intention of this project is to organize the themes of this book and illustrate some of the lessons so as to make application to our everyday life. So, let's jump into the various thoughts and ideas of Qoheleth-The Preacher.

ECCLESIASTES 1

> [1] *The words of the Teacher, son of David, king in Jerusalem:*
>
> [2] *"Meaningless! Meaningless!" says the Teacher. "Utterly meaningless! Everything is meaningless."*
>
> [3] *What do people gain from all their labors at which they toil under the sun?* [4] *Generations come and generations go, but the earth remains forever.* [5] *The sun rises and the sun sets, and hurries back to where it rises.* [6] *The wind blows to the south and turns to the north; round and round it goes, ever returning on its course.* [7] *All streams flow into the sea, yet the sea is never full. To the place the streams come from, there they return again.* [8] *All things are wearisome, more than one can say. The eye never has enough of seeing, nor the ear its fill of hearing.* [9] *What has been will be again, what has been done will be done again; there is nothing new under the sun.* [10] *Is there anything of which one can say, "Look! This is something new"? It was here already, long ago; it was here before our time.* [11] *No one remembers the former generations, and even those yet to come will not be remembered by those who follow them.*

The teacher opens up his discourse by making a statement about life in general. He calls everything *Hevel*. The Hebrew translation of this is "Breath" or more literally "Mere Breath." Some have likened it to the word "Nonsense." Others have attached the word "Meaningless." When viewed through the lens of life being a mere breath it is much more palatable to grasp the direction of the author. Since life is a mere breath, the key is to separate that which is truly important in life from that which is of passing value (like a breath). His statement could be rendered, "Everything is of passing value like a breath." This also communicates that life for all of us is short. In view of history we occupy a very small mark on the timeline of life.

John Piper demonstrates his understanding of the importance of seeking a life of value:

> A couple took early retirement from their jobs in the northeast five years ago when he was 59 and she was 51. Now they live in Punta Gorda, FL. where they cruise on their 30-foot trawler, play softball, and collect shells. At first when I read about them, I thought it might be a joke. A spoof on the American dream. But it wasn't. Tragically, this was the dream: Come to the end of your life—you're one and only precious God-given life—And let the last great work of your life, before you give an account to your Creator, be this: playing softball and collecting shells. Picture them before Christ at the great day of judgment: "Look Lord. See my shells!"

At a time when they could be spending their time making a difference, they chose to focus inwardly. By all accounts, this could very well be entitled, *The Meaningless Life*.

Looking at life from a purely outside view, we see that the nature we are surrounded by carries with it a cyclical behavior. And the life of man as a part of creation, also is cyclical in nature. This cyclical structure is seen in the following five examples:

Work - Although a person gains some semblance of completing a job, tomorrow is another day bringing more work to be done. Monday morning comes around with amazing rapidity.

It's a common practice for those in boot camp to be told to shovel a large pile of dirt from one place to another. It is also common for the men to return the next day and be ordered to shovel the dirt back to its original place.

This idea is further illustrated with the Greek mythological story of Sisyphus. Sisyphus was the king of Ephyra (Corinth). Because of his craftiness, deceit, and murder, he was destined by Zeus to roll a large boulder up a hill only to have it roll back down after nearing the top. This was his lot for all eternity. He understood the concept of "Meaningless." And just like Sisyphus, King Solomon notes that our work is never done.

Generations - People pass on, but God's creation remains. Magicians use a particular type of paper when wanting to wow the crowds. It's a very light paper that ignites extremely quickly. It gives off a flash of light, a miniscule amount of heat, some smoke, and then it's gone. In the timeline of history, a person, or a generation can be likened to that of tissue paper. In what seems like moments, they flash, give off a little *smoke and heat* and then they're gone!

The Sun - Considering the sun can put one in a very intimidated mood. Our sun is approximately 864,400 miles across. That's 109 times the size of our earth. It rises and sets (the earth actually rotates around it) and then rises again. It maintains an unbroken circular pattern.

Wind - The wind travels a different path. It goes back and forth but maintains a repeatable pattern as well. The strength of the wind is equally intimidating. Sometimes it seems like the wind is absent or completely still. At other times, the wind gets all of our attention. On Barrow Island, Australia, the 1996 Tropical Cyclone Olivia, brought gusts of wind eclipsing 253 miles per hour.

Rivers - Approximately seventy-one percent of our earth is covered by water and most of this is contained in our oceans. Rivers and lakes evaporate, turn to rain, and evaporate again. This is another cycle that never ends.

As a man who committed himself to experiencing everything he could, Solomon recognized that there is no end to discovery. As Ellen Parr has suggested, "The cure for boredom is curiosity. There is no cure for curiosity." Try as he may, man will never see all there is to see, and hear all there is to hear. The more man knows, the more he understands that he will never know it all. He opens doors only to find more doors to be opened.

In our hidden egocentric mind-set, we have the idea that if we don't see something, it does not exist. But certain things are in place and will remain in place regardless of them being seen or heard. They are permanent and independent of our recognition. Like opening a book to view a picture on the page. The picture was in the book before we saw it and did not depend on our discovery for its existence. The philosophical question, "If a tree falls in the forest and no one is there to hear it, does it still make a sound?" Solomon would answer a resounding "Yes!" If the tree was going to make a noise the noise will be there whether or not someone is present to hear it.

Eventually, those in the past will be forgotten, and try as they may, no one is able to see the future. Attempting to answer the following questions will demonstrate this reality:

1. Which team won the super bowl in 2002?
2. Who was the wealthiest person in America in 1993?
3. Who won the Miss Universe title in 2005?
4. Who won the world chess title in 2019?
5. In 2010 who won the Oscar for best actor?

The answers: 1-N.E. Patriots (20-17 over the St. Louis Rams) 2-Warren Buffet (8.3 Billion) 3- Amelia Vega (Dominican Republic) 4-Magnus Carlsen (Norway) 5-Jeff Bridges (Crazy Heart).

Unless you were a fan of the team, remember the headlines, or saw the event, chances are, you got them wrong. There is even a chance that you didn't venture a guess. These people reached the absolute pinnacle of success in their respective fields and yet within thirty years their names and accomplishments have sunk into oblivion. World records are constantly being broken. But if this world is *not* all you have these words won't sting as sharply or disappoint as greatly.

We don't want to be forgotten. We want our influence to be universal and last forever. So, we say things and do things we hope will have universal appeal and lasting results. But time marches on. Our impact on others is much smaller than we think and never goes as deep as we desire. We forget those who have come and gone, and we have no way of telling who is on the horizon and how long they will last before they too are forgotten.

So, what do we do with *the teacher's* opening discourse? How do we reconcile his statements with our view of our individual lives?

The first step is acceptance. We must realize that these claims are both universal and unrelenting. You cannot change one aspect of the cycle of nature any more than you can add one day of your life by worrying about it or focusing on it (Matthew 6:27). So, acceptance must be our initial mandate.

Next, we must realize that this world is not our home. We are here for a relatively short time. If this world is not our home, the aforementioned statements won't have a tendency to send us into a tailspin.

Also, we must set our minds on things above not on the temporal things of this life (Colossians. 3:2). As humans we must realize that we are not eternal, but we are immortal. That is to say that we have not lived forever, but we will live forever spiritually.

This idea of eternity is encapsulated in a story told by Hendrik Willem Van Loon in his book *The Story of Mankind*:

> High up in the North, in the land called Svithjod, there stands a rock. It is one hundred miles high and one hundred miles wide. Once every thousand years a little bird comes to this rock to sharpen its beak. When the rock has thus been worn away, then a single day of eternity will have gone by.

Lastly, we must realize that God has given us two very valuable gifts, but eternity on earth is not one of them. God has given each of us the opportunity to spend our eternal existence (after we die) with Him in heaven. Someone has rightly said, "You came with nothing. You leave with nothing. But you can send it on ahead."

This idea is illustrated by Tom and Jennifer when they made arrangements to move from New York to California. They had packed all their belongings into a rental truck. The truck was to drive to the west coast, and after finishing some business, they would drive their car a few days later. Tom noted, "Our treasure is not with us, but we will own it once again when we arrive at our final destination."

Along with spending all of eternity with Him, God has given us the present. We are not promised tomorrow, and yesterday has already faded into a memory. The measure of who we are is seen in how we deal with our todays.

In Alice Gray's collection of stories "Stories for the Heart" we find the following writing of Brother Jeremiah emphasizing the importance of living in the gift of the present:

> If I had my life to live over again, I'd try to make more mistakes next time. I would relax. I would limber up. I would be sillier than I have been this trip. I know a very few things I would take seriously. I would take more trips. I would climb more mountains, swim more rivers, and watch more sunsets. I would do more walking and looking. I would eat more ice cream and fewer beans. I would have more actual troubles and fewer imaginary ones. You see, I have one of those who lives prophylactically and sensibly and sanely hour after hour, day after day. Oh, I've had my moments: and if I had to do it over again, I'd have more of them. In fact, I'd try to have nothing else. Just moments, one after another, instead of living so many years ahead each day. I've been one of those people who never go anywhere without a thermometer, a hot water bottle, a gargle, a raincoat, aspirin and a parachute. If I had to do it over again, I would go places, do things, and travel lighter than I have. If I had my life to live over, I would ride on more merry-go-rounds—pick more daisies.

We have the promise of eternity after death, but have the gift of the present here and now.

> **¹² I, the Teacher, was king over Israel in Jerusalem.**
> **¹³ I applied my mind to study and to explore by wisdom all that is done under the heavens. What a heavy burden God has laid on mankind!**
> **¹⁴ I have seen all the things that are done under the sun; all of them are meaningless, a chasing after the wind.**
> **¹⁵ What is crooked cannot be straightened; what is lacking cannot be counted.**

Again, Solomon states his position as King over Israel in Jerusalem. This tells the reader that he is in position to explore. Nothing by way of finances, time, or authority stand in the way of him learning all he desires to learn about. The kingdom was secure, prospering, and free from war, giving him the freedom to turn his attention in any direction he desired. He chose to pursue wisdom gained by experience.

Solomon did not sit idly by waiting for the world to come to him. He pursued it with all the vigor of a starving man at a Christmas banquet.

He saw men endlessly working, striving, gaining, and losing yet continually pursuing more of what they believe will fulfill them. Life viewed this way is seen as a burden. The desire for more is deeply rooted in the heart of man, planted there by Almighty God.

John D. Rockefeller was the first billionaire in the United States, and at one time, the wealthiest person in the world. He was once asked by a reporter, "How much money is enough?" and Rockefeller replied, "Just a little bit more."

In like manner, a farmer made the comment about the possession of land. He said, "I don't want all the land in the world, just what comes into contact with mine."

With the idea that a man's life is a mere breath, Solomon also recognizes that the pursuits of men are just a vapor. The king investigated ALL the works of man and came to three conclusions:

1. Nothing that comes from man's hands lasts forever. The illustration is seen by placing one's hand in a bucket of water. After withdrawing it and looking for the hole, one sees how much permanence his life carries.

2. You can't undo what has been done. Like trying to grab the notes from a trumpet and bring them back, you cannot reverse things that have occurred.

"Do over" is a common call of children, when disputing a call while competing in sports. But life doesn't give you a "Do over." When the present moves into the category of the past, it washes away not to be seen again. *You can't step in the same river twice* is an accurate description of life's experiences. Class reunions are exciting and fun and much reminiscing is engaged in. Stories are told, and friends are re-acquainted, but the truth is, you can visit the past, but you can't re-live the past.

3. You cannot know the future and you cannot count what is not there. (Don't count your chickens before they hatch!) It is useless to pursue that which cannot be caught or doesn't exist. Reality is in fact, the only reality we have.

The Psychic hotline was a business that made great claims of being able to disclose a person's past as well as predict their future. Ironically, in 1998 they filed for bankruptsy with $26 million in liabilities. Despite all their claims this is something they should have seen coming.

ECCLESIASTES 2

I said to myself, "Come now, I will test you with pleasure to find out what is good." But that also proved to be meaningless. [2] "Laughter," I said, "is madness. And what does pleasure accomplish?" [3] I tried cheering myself with wine, and embracing folly—my mind still guiding me with wisdom. I wanted to see what was good for people to do under the heavens during the few days of their lives. [4] I undertook great projects: I built houses for myself and planted vineyards. [5] I made gardens and parks and planted all kinds of fruit trees in them. [6] I made reservoirs to water groves of flourishing trees. [7] I bought male and female slaves and had other slaves who were born in my house. I also owned more herds and flocks than anyone in Jerusalem before me. [8] I amassed silver and gold for myself, and the treasure of kings and provinces. I acquired male and female singers, and a harem as well—the delights of a man's heart. [9] I became greater by far than anyone in Jerusalem before me. In all this my wisdom stayed with me.

[10] I denied myself nothing my eyes desired; I refused my heart no pleasure. My heart took delight in all my labor, and this was the reward for all my toil. [11] Yet when I surveyed all that my hands had done and what I had toiled to achieve, everything was meaningless, a chasing after the wind; nothing was gained under the sun.

Solomon seems to be a "round peg" in search of a "round hole." His search caused him to develop a *Myopic disorder*. That is to say, he centered his thinking around himself. No less than thirty-nine times in this brief section, he uses the words, "I, My, Me," and "Myself." He was motivated by self-fulfillment. *What is there that I can do, see, and experience, that will bring me pleasure and fulfillment?* He tried various avenues in this pursuit. His motivation would fit nicely into the age-old heresy, "God wants me to be happy."

You'll notice that his pursuit of fulfillment falls neatly into nine categories: Laughter, wine, folly, activity, money, music (entertainment), sex, wisdom, and accolades. Without a great stretch of the imagination, we can see him changing gears as he tried one thing after another in order to see what worked best to fill this void in his life. This is not unlike so many people we see today. However, due to his great wealth and freedom, the process of obtaining wisdom was accelerated greatly.

Laughter was engaged in as he held an audience for comedians, jesters, and clowns. His version of a *laugh track* was probably engaged in with a room full of people who exploded with laughter at the slightest offering of humor.

When external pleasure dried up, he turned to an inner stimulant to bring a smile to his face. The finest wines the kingdom had to offer were ingested by him and those in his company and the effects were noted.

Folly is aligned with laughter but is built on foolish behavior. There is no real purpose behind it, and it seems to carry with it the idea of occupying time. You might call it silly or foolhardy behavior. Seeing how close you can stand on the edge of a cliff, concealing oneself and jumping out to scare people, or competing to see who can balance a tall set of plates the longest are examples of what we would label folly.

When these ventures failed to produce lasting effects, Solomon turned to projects. He built things and looked for fulfillment in accomplishments. He tried cooperating with nature to make things grow in a more productive way. This was done in gardening as well as fruit trees. He built an irrigation process for his trees and crops.

He also got involved with human propagation with slaves and experimented with birth planning. Along with this he experimented with cattle to enlarge his herds as well.

When these projects ran their course not bringing the desired long-lasting results, he turned to money and grew his financial empire with gold, silver, cattle, and land. It is estimated that if his wealth was converted in value to today's money, he would be worth well over 100 billion dollars.

If an individual possessed any special ability to entertain, it could easily be imagined that he would be summoned to the court of Solomon. Singers, dancers, musical performers would all be found sharing their gifts with the king. New songs and musical instruments were all brought in for Solomon's review and pleasure.

Part of his wealth was used to purchase women for sexual pleasure. And all during this time, he kept his wits about him and continued in his observations.

There was no limit to what Solomon saw and what he gathered sought to experience. If he saw something that he liked, he purchased it, experimented with it, or experienced it.

Still, in all his doing and getting, observing, and experiencing he was unable to maintain a firm grip on satisfaction. Something was missing! Solomon suffered with an internal void he could not fill.

The questions we must wrestle with are how many different cars can one drive? How much effort should be invested in emptying the store shelves and filling our own? How much is really enough? Both counting the stars or reaching for them would take a lifetime. Accolades, fame and things only increase our desire for more of the same and will serve only to drive us to the next thrill or experience, along the avenue of pleasure.

The danger in all of this is the possibility of engaging in self- destructive behavior. This is seen in the lives of Whitney Houston, River Phoenix, Heath Ledger, Amy Winehouse, Michael Jackson, and a host of other celebrities. They held the world in their hands and it only served to roll over them in a crushing conclusion.

Wing suit flying falls squarely in the category of those involved in self-destructive behavior. In an effort to achieve the ultimate adrenalin rush, these thrill seekers jump from a plane, tall building, or cliff, and glide for as long as possible before deploying their chutes. To heighten the excitement even more, some flyers defy the elements by flying through rock openings, under bridges, and clipping balloons on the edge of a precipice. If all goes well, the thrill is gained, the landing accomplished, and a great story is built. But it doesn't always go well.

It was August 13th, 2013, near Les Grandes Otanes, Switzerland. Forty-two-year old stuntman Marc Sutton lost his life while wingsuit flying. Jumping from a helicopter at 10,000 feet, Sutton descended at more than 150 miles per hour before crashing into the side of a mountain. He was killed instantly.

Others see no hope and take their lives somehow reasoning that life will not get any better. Depression, psychosis, and a cry for help are contributing factors. Curt Cobain, Ernest Hemingway, Marilyn Monroe, Robin Williams, and Vincent Van Gogh are among some of the most famous personalities who concluded that to end their life would be better than to live in a state of hopelessness.

Solomon evaluated all that his hands had accomplished and came to the conclusion, that as great as it was, it still carried no lasting value. In the big picture of it all, it still lasted no more than a mere breath.

> *12Then I turned my thoughts to consider wisdom, and also madness and folly. What more can the king's successor do than what has already been done? 13I saw that wisdom is better than folly, just as light is better than darkness. 14The wise have eyes in their heads, while the fool walks in the darkness; but I came to realize that the same fate overtakes them both.*
>
> *15Then I said to myself, "The fate of the fool will overtake me also. What then do I gain by being wise?" I said to myself, "This too is meaningless." 16For the wise, like the fool, will not be long remembered; the days have already come when both have been forgotten. Like the fool, the wise too must die!*

The king now turns to the intellectual side of things. He evaluated wisdom, madness, and folly, and did not even bother with a conclusion regarding madness. He simply felt it was not worth considering.

It is easy to imagine him sitting back on his throne, giving a heavy sigh while reflecting back on all he had done. He concluded that he had done it all. In a soft way, he made the claim that no one following him will accomplish what he had done.

Then the teacher jumps back to the subject at hand-wisdom. He states that wisdom is so much better than foolishness. He placed both of these subjects at opposite ends of the spectrum and makes the analogy that just as light is better than darkness, so is wisdom better than foolishness.

It is similar to the quote attributed to Beatrice Kaufman. While at a tavern Mrs. George S. Kaufman urges a noted theatrical figure to accept the movie offers being tendered him. "Listen, and take my advice," she urged. "Don't overlook the money part of it. I've been poor and I've been rich. Rich is better!" King Solomon would have paraphrased this by saying, "Take my advice, I've been foolish, and I've been wise. Being wise is better!"

The ability to see, discern, and evaluate are only found in the wise. Fools stumble through life and are constantly falling and having to recover. After these comments he comes to the "And yet…" part of his thinking. It must be kept in mind that death is no respecter of persons, position, the wise, or the foolish. Father time is undefeated, and no one gets out of here alive!

At this point, we are faced with the universal question: *What then?* In all our are doing and getting and in all our activity we must have in the recesses of our mind that no matter who we are or what we've done, one day, our life will in fact, end. *What then?* And what comes next will be all that matters.

When you only consider the end of life it naturally gravitates toward despair. Life is a vapor and Solomon notes that in the end, we all go to the graveyard. He stresses that people's memory of you will be short lived and that death is the common destination for all. This cannot draw you to anything, but depression and he alludes to the idea that we already see the short-lived memories in the lives of those who have gone before us. This leads him to verses 17-20.

> *¹⁷ So I hated life, because the work that is done under the sun was grievous to me. All of it is meaningless, a chasing after the wind. ¹⁸ I hated all the things I had toiled for under the sun, because I must leave*

them to the one who comes after me. ¹⁹ And who knows whether that person will be wise or foolish? Yet they will have control over all the fruit of my toil into which I have poured my effort and skill under the sun. This too is meaningless. ²⁰ So my heart began to despair over all my toilsome labor under the sun.

In all of the teachings of Jesus, He only labels one man a "fool." In the parable of the rich fool (Luke 12:16-21) Jesus notes the financial success of a particular man. The man is not labeled a fool because he couldn't make money, didn't work hard, or plan ahead. He is called a fool because he equates financial success with long life, and he disregards spiritual matters. He knows he has a soul but is living as if he doesn't.

Solomon sees the futility of all he has accomplished and recognizes that his view of the entire situation is leading him in a downward spiral mentally and emotionally. He is troubled that his death will lead to a lack of control over all his accomplishments and that he must leave everything to one who may not handle things well. Grievous, meaningless, and a hopeless pursuit are buzzwords for how he is feeling. He is saddened by the reality that you really "Can't take it with you!" and that our grip on everything, must eventually be loosed.

This is pictured in the story of a miserly man who was on his deathbed. He told his wife that he believed that it was in fact, possible to "take it with you." He instructed her to take a good bit of his gold and put it in his jacket just before he passed on. She did so and when the old miser died and went to heaven, he found himself wearing the same jacket. When he reached into the pockets, he discovered that the gold was still there. He was elated and ran about heaven showing all the saints the gold that he had taken with him. "Look" he said, "I did it! I did it! I took it with me!"

Two angels were standing nearby watching the man run around showing everyone his gold. One turned to the other and said, "Who's the new guy with all that road pavement in his pockets?"

Regarding work, Solomon concludes that when all you live for, long for, think of, and dream about is work you will come to the conclusion that life is meaningless. "What difference does it all make anyway?" This will be a question loudly ringing in your ears.

> *21 For a person may labor with wisdom, knowledge and skill, and then they must leave all they own to another who has not toiled for it. This too is meaningless and a great misfortune. 22 What do people get for all the toil and anxious striving with which they labor under the sun? 23 All their days their work is grief and pain; even at night their minds do not rest. This too is meaningless.*

If all your life is centered around work, you will feel empty when your work is done. Even though you put your best effort into it, and it occupies your mind, day and night, it will amount to nothing in your heart if that's all you have. Solomon is taking a horizontal look at life. He only sees life in the here and now. He is not taking into account accomplishments that may work for the betterment of others in the future.

A key question must be dealt with in order to sidestep this pessimistic attitude: Is the world a better place because you're in it? Solomon missed it due to his myopic attitude. His thoughts were centered around himself, and so he concluded that all his activity, advancements and discoveries would follow him to the grave.

Perhaps those who have made some unique and helpful discoveries wondered if their contributions were worthwhile. But today, we are thankful for: Penicillin, air conditioning, the computer, transportation, pasteurization, the aspirin, morphine, the heart valve, the telephone, and an endless list of other things. Those who invented these things are long gone. Many of us do not remember who did what, but we can't forget that it was done and we are quick to enjoy the efforts of those who brought these things our way.

> *24 A person can do nothing better than to eat and drink and find satisfaction in their own toil. This too, I see, is from the hand of God, 25 for without him, who can eat or find enjoyment? 26 To the person who pleases him, God gives wisdom, knowledge and happiness, but to the sinner he gives the task of gathering and storing*

***up wealth to hand it over to the one who pleases God.
This too is meaningless, a chasing after the wind.***

In view of our inability to control the future and what others will do with the wealth we leave behind, Solomon turns to the gift of the present. For a second time, God is introduced into the equation. The first time (1:13) God is mentioned as one who has given the burden of continually seeking and exploring. Here God is seen as a generous benefactor who gives the ability to enjoy one's work, with eating and drinking. God is the one who gives wisdom, knowledge, and happiness.

VV24-26 - Basic activities are good and should be enjoyed. Eating, drinking, and working are things that should bring satisfaction. But we must keep in mind that even the enjoyment of these things comes at the hand of God. God brings blessings to those who strive to please Him.

A contrast is made between those who acknowledge God and the sinner. Those who follow God find satisfaction in their work, wisdom, and knowledge to enjoy their labor, and happiness in their life. To the sinner however belongs the task of working hard but then handing over their abundance to the one who pleases the Lord.

Those who are in rebellion against Him will find that everything they do and gather will slip through their hands, and they will not enjoy it the way they could. Those who miss God's mark are destined to look back on their life and activities and conclude that everything they worked for and chased after wasn't worth sweating over and possessing. God and God alone is the author of satisfaction, enjoyment, and fulfillment. Chuck Swindoll said it so well, "The happiest people I know are the ones who have learned how to hold everything loosely and have given the worrisome, stress-filled, fearful details of their lives into God's keeping."

ECCLESIASTES 3

¹There is a time for everything, and a season for every activity under the heavens: ² a time to be born and a time to die, a time to plant and a time to uproot, ³ a time to kill and a time to heal, a time to tear down and a time to build, ⁴ a time to weep and a time to laugh, a time to mourn and a time to dance, ⁵ a time to scatter stones and a time to gather them, a time to embrace and a time to refrain from embracing, ⁶ a time to search and a time to give up, a time to keep and a time to throw away, ⁷ a time to tear and a time to mend, a time to be silent and a time to speak, ⁸ a time to love and a time to hate, a time for war and a time for peace.

VV.1-8 - In 1965, a band called *The Byrds* recorded a song written by Pete Seeger that was greatly embraced by both young and old. It was titled *Turn, Turn, Turn*. Though it was enjoyed by so many, few understood that the theme was derived from Ecclesiastes 3:1-8. "To everything there is a season..."

In this section Solomon stresses that life is meant to be lived in balance. In Genesis 1 and 2 we see God's desire for mankind. There were thirteen elements in the garden depicting God's design for us.

These are the elements God orchestrated enabling man to live a balanced life:

1. A healthy diet: Genesis 1:29
2. Worship: Genesis 2:1-3

3. Work: Genesis 2:15
4. Abstinence/Discipline: Genesis 2:17
5. Interpersonal relationships: Genesis 1:27-28, 2:18, 2:24
6. Study: Genesis 2:19-20
7. Rest: Genesis 2:21
8. Art: Genesis 2:23
9. Sunshine: Genesis 1:3, 2:25
10. Play: Genesis 1:28
11. Obedience: Genesis 2:15
12. Fresh Air: Genesis 2:15
13. Exercise: Genesis 2:15

A balanced life was designed by God and stressed in this passage by King Solomon. Seasons come and go. Wisdom will help you evaluate and recognize what season you are in and empower you to act appropriately. There are several ways of distinguishing and categorizing the various seasons life brings us.

Some seasons are positive aspects of life bringing with them joy and happiness. (birth, harvesting, embracing, love, peace). Other seasons are negative and bring with them sobriety and sorrow (death, loss, war).

Some seasons are long and working through them takes a great deal of time. Seasons such as planting, healing, building, mourning, and searching give us the idea that these are longer processes than others such as uprooting, laughing, embracing etc.

Some season are individualized (birth, death, weeping, laughing, silence, love, hate etc.) Other seasons call for mutual involvement and are more intentional (building, embracing, searching, war, and perhaps dancing).

Some seasons are physical (birth, death, killing, healing, tearing down, dancing, gathering, scattering, embracing, searching, discarding, tearing, mending, warring).

Other seasons fall into the emotional category (weeping, laughing, mourning, refraining from embracing, loving, hating).

It must be noted that one season seems to be a combination of physical and emotional outpouring (dancing).

Some activities are under our control and call for engagement at our discretion (killing/healing, tearing down/building up, scattering/

gathering, embracing/refraining, keeping/throwing away, tearing/ mending, being silent/speaking, waging war/living in peace).

Other activities are beyond our control. They are part of our lives and they happen without our influence (birth/death, planting/ reaping season, events we cry over/those we laugh about, events we mourn about/those we dance about).

Taken as couplets this section gives us instruction on balancing life.

Birth/Death: These are inevitable issues of life. One is to be celebrated, and the other draws us to sorrow. When a new life arrives, it is a call for great rejoicing. But balance is embraced with the recognition that one day that little one will pass away. We must not be taken unaware of this reality of life: death follows life, but new life also follows death.

Planting/Uprooting: The three most common New Testament metaphors that are used regarding the Christian are that the Christian is a soldier, an athlete, and a farmer. Here is a reference using the illustration of a farmer. Some things must be done to foster new life and growth. Other things must be done away with. It is important to know when it is time to plant new things and when it is time to get rid of the things that are harmful, non-productive, or have outlived their usefulness.

Ephesians 4:20-24 commands us to "Uproot" that which is sinful in our lives and to "Plant" that which is God-honoring: [20] "But you did not learn Christ in this way, [21] if indeed you have heard Him and have been taught in Him, just as truth is in Jesus, [22] that, in reference to your former manner of life, you lay aside the old self, which is being corrupted in accordance with the lusts of deceit, [23] and that you be renewed in the spirit of your mind, [24] and put on the new self, which in *the likeness of* God has been created in righteousness and holiness of the truth."

Killing/Healing: This is a difficult concept to grasp as Christians. We understand and embrace the concept of healing, but is there a time for the Christian to kill? Regarding murder, no (You shall not murder-Exodus 20:13). But if the analogy is to be made that there are ideas, temptations, attitudes, and behaviors that we would do well to kill, then putting them to death can be an acceptable choice.

This idea can be seen in Romans 8:13, "for if you are living according to the flesh, you must die; but if by the Spirit you are putting to death the deeds of the body, you will live."

Likewise, healing is needed physically, emotionally, relationally, socially, and in a myriad of other ways all of which can be voluntarily engaged in by the followers of Christ.

Tearing Down/Building: This too can be seen to be addressing the physical as well as the spiritual. There are times when physical buildings are no longer needed and should be done away with. There are other times when programs and methods are no longer effective, and they too must be put away or "torn down." Times change and seasons end for programs and behaviors. The methods used years ago may not be effective today for reaching people for Christ. Music, fashions, and programs must change with the times if we are to affect the culture we are presently living in. This is not to say that our doctrine or message changes. But it is to understand that the method of sharing the message must change to be relevant to the culture we are living in.

Thomas Jefferson phrased it this way, "In matters of style, swim with the current; in matters of principle, stand like a rock."

In 1 Corinthians 13:11, the Apostle Paul states, "When I was a child, I used to speak like a child, think like a child, reason like a child; when I became a man, I did away with childish things."

In a way, He is saying that there is a time to tear down and a time to build up.

Weeping/Laughing: Life brings with it issues that bring tears to our eyes. Other issues bring laughter to our hearts. Each is appropriate in particular settings. We do not expect much laughter to be experienced at a funeral nor do we expect downcast hearts at a wedding or graduation. Our times of celebration need to be balanced with the understanding that difficult times are inevitable. Likewise, we need to know that although our times of mourning are heart wrenching, laughter in time, will return. Psalm 30:5b tells us, "Weeping may last for the night, but a shout of joy *comes* in the morning."

In the Hebrew tradition, the Seder meal included bitter herbs in a special pitcher. This was passed around and all in attendance partook of the bitter drink. The purpose was to remind them of the bitterness of Egyptian slavery, and the fact that life does contain a certain amount of bitterness.

Mourning/Dancing: This follows the same idea of weeping and laughing. There will come seasons in all of our lives when our hearts are in deep despair. Without question, the loss of a loved one falls into this category. If we live long enough, all of us will experience the loss of someone close to us and experience a season of mourning. St. John of the Cross has termed this, "The dark night of the soul."

There are moments during this time when we feel that the darkness will never end, and we are destined to a lifetime of sadness. But Solomon reminds us that days of dancing will come. The sun will shine again, and a melody will return to our hearts.

Jesus spoke to this issue when He said, "These things I have spoken to you, so that in Me you may have peace. In the world you have tribulation, but take courage; I have overcome the world" (John 16:33).

Gathering/Scattering: Gathering and scattering are terms that can be used regarding objects, ideas, or people. During harvest, seeds are gathered. But during planting, those same seeds are scattered, and the stage is set for future harvesting.

The educational years in a person's life are the time for gathering. Different ideas are presented and the wise student soaks in all they can. But upon graduation, the time comes to scatter the knowledge that has been gathered. To hold onto wisdom and not share it is tantamount to stealing and can be said to be a waste of a good education.

This was seen in the life of James Crichton. Crichton was probably the greatest prodigy that ever lived. He was born in 1560 in Scotland. At thirteen, he was given a bachelor of arts degree. At seventeen, he was awarded a masters' of arts degree. At nineteen, he went about Europe, challenging all the learned men to meet him in open forum. He boasted he could answer any question in any field of learning, speaking in any one of ten languages. He confounded his auditors not only with his remarkable knowledge but with the facility of his expression.

He was literally a human encyclopedia, knowing all about everything.

Not only did Crichton startle the world with his feats of mental agility, but he was equally proficient in nimbleness and strength of body.

He was a painter, a singer, a dancer, a horseman, a card-player- apparently equally skilled in all the social and fine arts.

Crichton was killed at the age of 22 by a drunken prince whom he was employed to tutor.

However, with all his physical and mental abilities the Admirable Crichton was as helpless as an inanimate library when it came to putting his vast knowledge to use. He accomplished no useful thing during his short life, and his biographers doubt whether a longer life would have made any difference. He invented nothing, he formulated no new theory, not a single noble thought bears his name. His mind was like the wax of a recording phonograph; it received impressions and reproduced what was recorded. He is a prime example of one who gathered but never scattered.

The church of Christ is not to be this way. We are to meet to gain Gospel knowledge, ideas, and resources. Then we are dismissed to scatter the good news to all we encounter. It's similar to a sports team. The practice field is the place of gathering. The playing field is the place of scattering our skills to bring about a victory.

The story is told about Ignacy Jan Paderewski, the famous composer-pianist. He understood the concept of gathering for the purpose of scattering. He was scheduled to perform at a great concert hall in America. Present in the audience that evening was a mother with her fidgety nine-year-old son. Weary of waiting, he squirmed constantly in his seat. His mother was in hopes that her boy would be encouraged to practice the piano if he could just hear the immortal Paderewski at the keyboard. So, against his wishes, the boy had come.

As she turned to talk with friends, her son could stay seated no longer. He slipped out of his seat, strangely drawn to the ebony concert grand Steinway and its leather-tufted stool on the huge stage floored with blinding lights.

Without much notice from the sophisticated audience, the boy sat down at the stool, staring wide-eyed at the black and white keys. He placed his small, trembling fingers in the right location and began to play *Chopsticks*.

The roar of the crowd was hushed as hundreds of frowning faces turned in his direction. Irritated and embarrassed, they began to shout: "Get that boy away from there!" "Who'd bring a kid that young in here?" "Where's his mother?" "Somebody stop him!"

Backstage, the master overheard the sounds out front and quickly put together in his mind what was happening. Hurriedly, he grabbed his coat and rushed toward the stage. Without one word of announcement, he stepped behind the boy, reached around both sides, and began to improvise a counter melody to harmonize and enhance *Chopsticks*. As the two of them played together, Paderewski kept whispering in the boy's ear; "Keep going. Don't quit, son. Keep on playing .... Don't stop....Don't quit." All his years of gathering were now invested in scattering.

Embracing/Refraining from Embracing: This is a concept that is readily seen in many areas of our world.

As parents, there are times when our children desperately need to be embraced and held in our arms. There are other times when strict discipline needs to be administered. When we get them confused or engage in one to the exclusion of the other, we run the risk of developing our children into either egocentric or calloused adults.

Employers know there is a time to encourage good performance and a time to penalize slackness. A good coach understands when it is time to motivate and when it is time to castigate.

Mature Christians understand that there must be a balance in our dealings with others between grace and judgment. Grace overextended may lead to easy believism. Harsh judgment on the other hand can lead to legalism. Our goal is to welcome the sinner but not affirm the sin.

Searching/Abandoning the Search: It is very hard for us to think of a time when searching for something of value is to be stopped. We have the backdrop of Luke 15 to encourage us to keep searching. The lost coin, lost sheep, and lost son stand as examples of the rewards of a continued search. History is replete with examples of people who achieved success simply by *pressing on*. Thomas Edison stands as an example of this. It is said that he failed over one thousand times to invent his version of the light bulb.

Yet this is balanced by those who spent their entire lives chasing something they never caught. There are times when what we are looking for is not to be found. Over the centuries countless treasure seekers have spent their lives in search of the Holy Grail. Sasquatch, the Loch Ness Monster, and Pegasus, may serve as examples of searches that would be best given up.

It takes a certain level of wisdom to know when to press on in the search and when to spend our energies in other pursuits.

Keep/Throw Away: If you've even viewed an episode of the television show *Hoarders* you will have no trouble in applying this adage. Old newspapers, empty boxes, crusts from a pizza party are all common items found in the homes of hoarders. Somehow, they have attached value to these items and cannot emotionally and physically detach themselves from them. But this couplet speaks of the issue of value. Things that have value need to be kept. Those that hold no lasting value should be discarded.

George H. Kaufman found a five-dollar bill on the sidewalk when he was eleven years old. Fortune had so smiled upon him that little George determined never again to look up, but to always look down. Over his lifetime he found 25,613 buttons, 21 umbrellas, 2,361 pins, $1,113.52, and a bent back. But he missed his wife's face, sunsets, birds, trees, and the stars. Kaufman threw away the things he couldn't keep and missed viewing all the things that last forever.

Pictures of loved ones, gifts from special people, wedding rings, family movies, and legal papers are all examples of items that carry real value and should be kept.

Jesus talked about the pursuit of things of value when he told the parable of hidden treasure:

"The kingdom of heaven is like a treasure hidden in the field, which a man found and hid *again*; and from joy over it he goes and sells all that he has and buys that field" (Matthew 13:44).

Further, Jesus makes a statement of pursuing things of value rather than those that do not last, when He said in Matthew 6:19-21: "Do not store up for yourselves treasures on earth, where moth and rust destroy, and where thieves break in and steal. But store up for yourselves treasures in heaven, where neither moth nor rust destroys, and where thieves do not break in or steal; for where your treasure is, there your heart will be also."

As followers of Christ, we have items that hold real value to us because of what they represent. The cross, a certificate of baptism, and the Word of God are examples of items to be kept. Hold on to them and enjoy the value they represent.

Tearing/Mending: Though Solomon may be speaking about something physical, this couplet could equally be applied to the interpersonal relationships and the behavior we engage in.

In general, the relationships we have will ether build us up or drag us down. We will either be nurtured and growing because of the relationships we've built, or we will find ourselves truncated in our growth as a person also due to those with whom we surround ourselves.

Paroled criminals are prohibited from keeping company with other paroled criminals because there is a tendency to spiral in a downward direction. This is where relational tearing should be administered.

The Bible says it this way, "Do not be deceived: Bad company corrupts good morals." (1 Corinthians. 15:33)

The instances or broken relationships is long. Marriages, friendships, family members, and even business relationships can all be estranged and dissolved.

When relationships are in need of mending, time, desire, humility, and intentionality are required. It takes a great deal of effort to initiate the words like, "I was wrong. Please forgive me" or "I'm sorry."

In the New Testament we witness this happen between Paul and Barnabas. Acts 15:36-40 tells us,

> [36]*After some days Paul said to Barnabas, Let us return and visit the brethren in every city in which we proclaimed the word of the Lord, and see how they are.* [37] *Barnabas wanted to take John, called Mark, along with them also.* [38] *But Paul kept insisting that they should not take him along who had deserted them in Pamphylia and had not gone with them to the work.* [39] *And there occurred such a sharp disagreement that they separated from one another, and Barnabas took Mark with him and sailed away to Cyprus.* [40] *But Paul chose Silas and left, being committed by the brethren to the grace of the Lord.*

Their disagreement was sharp, and their relationship was

temporarily severed.

But thankfully, mending did take place. We are not informed of all the details, but eventually, Paul reached back out to Barnabas and their relationship was renewed. In 2 Timothy 4:11 he calls for help from Mark. "Only Luke is with me. Pick up Mark and bring him with you, for he is useful to me for service."

Regarding his relationship with Barnabas, Paul writes in Galatians 2:1, "Then after an interval of fourteen years I went up again to Jerusalem with Barnabas, taking Titus along also."

Along with relationships, there is behavior that we should either mend or sever from us. By mending a behavior, it can be said that there are certain godly activities we used to be engaged in, but no longer do so. Somehow over time, we've gotten away from them and we need to re-introduce them into our lives. Church attendance, daily devotional time, giving, prayer, and committed fellowship can be examples of behavior we formally engaged in that we need to mend, or get back to.

Conversely, there are certain behaviors, attitudes, and thoughts that we would do well to tear from our lives. Any of those that run contrary to the word and will of God fit into this category.

Philippians 4:8 instructs us, "Finally, brethren, whatever is true, whatever is honorable, whatever is right, whatever is pure, whatever is lovely, whatever is of good repute, if there is any excellence and if anything is worthy of praise, dwell on these things."

In 1 Peter 2:12 we find this admonition, "Keep your behavior excellent among the Gentiles, so that in the thing in which they slander you as evildoers, they may because of your good deeds, as they observe them, glorify God in the day of visitation."

Whether it's regarding relationships or behavior, there is a time to mend and a time to tear away. A discerning mind is necessary to understand what, where, and when these are needed.

Being Silent/Speaking: Verse 7 recognizes a verbal season. Silence and speaking are controllable seasons that are called for as well. Wisdom helps us to know when to speak up and when to shut up.

There have been numerous pundits weighing in on the topic of the timing of communication. Among them is Thomas Edison who said, "You will have many opportunities in life to keep your mouth shut: You should take advantage of every one of them."

Mark Twain put it this way, "It's better to keep your mouth shut and appear stupid than open it and remove all doubt."

James 1:19 tells us, "This you know, my beloved brethren. But everyone must be quick to hear, slow to speak and slow to anger." Radio show host Larry King said, "I've never learned anything while talking."

Of course, there are times when we are wise to speak up. Our call is to speak up for the cause of Christ. Jesus last command, also known as the "Great Commission" is that we should go everywhere and share the Gospel.

There is a time to speak and a time to keep silent. Wisdom compels us to know which is at hand and to implement it in a timely manner.

Love/Hate: As followers of Christ, we have so many commands to love. Among others, recipients of our love include, our brothers and sisters (John 13:35), our enemies (Matthew 5:44), our Neighbors (Matthew 19:19), Our God (Mark 12:30), our enemies (Luke 6:27), and the law of God Psalm 119:97).

But when does hate become appropriate for those who name the name of Christ?

We are hard-pressed to find instances where God commands us to hate others, but hatred of sinful behavior abounds in His word.

Psalm 97:10, instructs us, "Hate evil, you who love the Lord, who preserves the souls of His godly ones; He delivers them from the hand of the wicked."

Also from the book of Psalms alone, we find a short list of behavior that is to be hated:

- Iniquities (Psalm 5:5)
- The assembly of evildoers (Psalm 26:5)
- The worship of vain idols (Psalm 31:6)
- Evil (Psalm 97:10)
- Double minded behavior (Psalm 119:113)

In short, we are instructed to love people, but hate any behavior that dishonors the Lord.

War/Peace: Perhaps Solomon left this last pair to serve as a creshendo—to wrap up all he has been saying. From a physical standpoint, war is the most dangerous position to be in and threats to destruction abound. It is a position to be avoided. Yet conflict is not always avoidable.

In Romans 12:28, we find this admonition: "If possible, so far as it depends on you, be at peace with all men." Here we understand that peace is to be pursued. But we also see that the road to peace may be roadblocked. Not everyone desires to be at peace with us. There are indeed some people, and nations that desire war rather than peace. Solomon concedes that there is a time for war even when we prefer peace.

> *[9] What do workers gain from their toil? [10] I have seen the burden God has laid on the human race.*

Solomon questions the value of work, yet sees man continue to strive, and reach for more. It is deep in a man's heart to be busy. Like ants who continually build we must fulfill this deep-seated desire to hunt and gather. More, bigger, and newer seem to be the mantra of the day.

A successful businessman was on vacation. One afternoon as he strolled along the shore, he came upon a fisherman who was busy cleaning his net. He asked the man about what he was doing, and the man told him, "I've caught a fish and after I clean my net, I'm going to take it home and cook it and enjoy it with my family." Immediately the business mind of the man kicked in. He said, "Well if you keep fishing, you'll catch another fish and you can sell that fish and then you can buy a bigger net." The man asked, "Why would I want to do that?" "Then you could catch more fish sell them and buy a bigger boat" the man responded. The fisherman asked, "And what good will that do?" The man countered, "Then you could hire other men to fish for you and you could sell more and more fish and eventually you'll have lots of money and you can retire and go home and enjoy life with your family." After a pause the fisherman looked at the visitor and said, "That's what I'm going to do tonight."

When a jig-saw puzzle of 5,000 pieces is completed, it brings great satisfaction. The feeling of accomplishment, the beauty of the picture, and the reward of a job well done are held in the forefront of one's mind. Yet after a period of time, the result is the same for each worker of the puzzle. Each piece is separated, and all the pieces go back in the box.

In all our busyness and striving to get ahead and obtain more, we must heed the command, "Be still, and know that I am God" (Psalm 46:10).

God clearly understands this. In the Hebrew culture it is commanded by God to honor the Sabbath and cease from work. Also, the Jews were commanded to set aside certain days for feasting and celebrating. Among those are, the Passover, The Day of Atonement, The Festival of Booths, and the Jewish New Year. These days of rest and celebration are not optional. God is saying, "You will rest! You will enjoy yourself!"

> *11 He has made everything beautiful in its time. He has also set eternity in the human heart; yet no one can fathom what God has done from beginning to end.*

We must never forget that God is in charge and He gives life order and balance. As the seasons change, leaves turn brown, fall off and the tree enters a season of dormancy. Then spring comes, and with it a lime green color is seen on the end of branches. As the leaves grow, their color turns to a dark green and the tree gives evidence of great life. The time is right for the tree to show its beauty.

The idea of eternity is deeply embedded in the heart of mankind. There is no end to the speculation about what happens after one dies. People are anxious to know about the hereafter. Because of this they will enlist the help of *Psychics, Mediums,* Tarot cards, and crystal balls to discover what lies in store for them and the condition of a loved one who has passed away.

I have always been amazed when I see a sign in a yard advertising a psychic and note the poor condition of their house and property. If they could tell the future can't they predict the stock market or the winner of the Kentucky Derby?

Numerous books have been written and stories have been told of those who have had a glimpse of the afterlife and have returned to share their experiences and each of these people find a sea of ears ready to take in every word regarding the here-after. Our hunger to know the unknown is insatiable.

But we must understand that God is still in charge of the present and the future—even eternity. He has chosen to give man a curious heart regarding the future yet has kept the answer from being completely clear even though we are given glimpses from His Word.

> [12] *I know that there is nothing better for people than to be happy and to do good while they live. [13] That each of them may eat and drink, and find satisfaction in all their toil—this is the gift of God. [14] I know that everything God does will endure forever; nothing can be added to it and nothing taken from it. God does it so that people will fear him. [15] Whatever is has already been, and what will be has been before; and God will call the past to account.*

The pursuit of happiness is imbedded deep within our hearts. But at the same time, we must understand that our desire for happiness must not be done at the expense of another person's happiness. There is currently a misguided philosophy among Christians that, "God wants me to be happy." This sounds like a godly biblical idea, but the Scriptures do not bear it out. It's simply a God-sounding way of saying, "I'm going to do what I want." And this includes indulging in whatever sinful pleasure they choose. However, you'll notice that those who adhere to this philosophy feel that it only applies to them. When a person states, "God wants me to be happy, so... I'm divorcing you, getting drunk, having an affair, stealing from the company..." (you fill in the blank), they are in essence saying, "God wants me to be happy, but your happiness is not His concern."

Biblically, do you see happiness as the hallmark of the followers of God? If you look at the heroes of the faith, do you see happiness at the top of the list of life-characteristics? What you do see in the lives of those who are honored by God is the over-arching penchant toward holiness. God calls us to be holy! (1 Peter 1:16) What you will find is that one can seek happiness and not be found to be holy. But the pursuit of holiness will often lead to happiness.

Solomon couples happiness with doing good. In essence he is saying doing good or living rightly is directly related to happiness.

Do good, be holy and you will find happiness.

Having the ability to arrive at the end of the day knowing that you have lived well, done rightly, and worked hard is a gift of God and is rewarded with satisfaction and happiness. A mind and body spent in an admirable effort naturally brings one to peaceful rest.

Yet we know that our work does not endure. Someday our accomplishments will burn, rot, decay, dissolve, or be forgotten. We also understand that whatever God does endures until He commands it to be gone. The by-product of His hand is always perfection. It does not need to be corrected. When we truly see the work of God and understand the perfection of it, we can't help but honor and revere Him.

The intimidating beauty of the Grand Canyon, the immenseness of the great Sequoia trees in California, the gracefulness of an eagle in flight, the magnificence of the human body, and the immenseness of the universe, lead us to bow in reverence, applaud in honor, and shake our head in amazement.

Romans 1:20 speaks to this, "For since the creation of the world God's invisible qualities—his eternal power and divine nature—have been clearly seen, being understood from what has been made, so that people are without excuse." It's been rightly said, "All creation is an outstretched finger pointing to God."

God's work is complete and perfect. Nothing needs to be added to it. Our contribution to God's creation would do nothing but mar it. It is tantamount to touching up the Mona Lisa.

When considering the creative hand of God, what we see in the present is not something that is newly created. It is something that is newly discovered. We as humans are not creating anything new, we're just discovering what is already there.

And so it is with truth. Truth is not something that exists because we created it. We don't vote on something making it true. It is not made by consensus. Truth is something that already exists which we discover.

Before moving onto another point, Solomon draws a light conclusion to this section by adding the point of accountability. *God will call the past to account.*

He encourages his listeners to be happy and do good, to eat, drink, and find satisfaction in their work. But he also emphasizes that the watchful eye of the Lord will draw judgment upon the actions of man.

Next, the King seems to say, "And another thing..."

> ^{16} *And I saw something else under the sun:*
> *In the place of judgment—wickedness was there, ^{17}I*
> *said to myself, "God will bring into judgment both the*
> *righteous and the wicked, for there will be a time for*
> *every activity, a time to judge every deed."*

Where justice and judgment should be evident, Solomon saw man acting wickedly. Today as in the days of Solomon, wickedness seems to be winning. Man's sin against man seems to forever be reaching new heights. Justice does not always triumph on earth. Bad things really do happen to good people!

Man's law is loaded with loopholes and exceptions.

Despite the overwhelming evidence, a criminal is set free simply because his Miranda rights were misstated. There are episodes of evidence tampering. The law of the land seems to be "Might makes right." Our general behavior is only a hair's-breath above the beasts. A parent kills their children and children kill their parents.

But in the end, it will be God who brings ultimate justice. No one and nothing that anyone has ever done will escape the judgment hand of God. He will bring justice to all.

In 1938 Italian Benito Mussolini said, "I'll hang God in Fascist Italy!" And they found Mussolini himself, hanging upside down from a steel beam, no life in his body.

Joseph Stalin said, "I'll erase the memory of God from Russia!" But now they curse Stalin's name and one cannot even find the place where he is buried.

Adolf Hitler sneered, "An anemic Jew called Jesus is not worthy of German worship!" And they found Hitler a smoking cinder in a German gutter.

The emperor Niro was one of the most well-known haters of Christianity and was responsible for the beheading of the Apostle Paul. Today we name our sons Paul and our dogs Nero.

The King continues this thought pattern when he states:

18 I also said to myself, "As for humans, God tests them so that they may see that they are like the animals. 19Surely the fate of human beings is like that of the animals; the same fate awaits them both: As one dies, so dies the other. All have the same breath; humans have no advantage over animals. Everything is meaningless. 20 All go to the same place; all come from dust, and to dust all return. 21 Who knows if the human spirit rises upward and if the spirit of the animal goes down into the earth?"

Life is full of tests. These tests reveal to us who and how we really are at the core of our being. Our lives are like overfilled glasses, when shaken (tested) whatever is inside comes out. Albert Einstein said it this way, "Adversity introduces a man to himself." Most tests in life reveal that the one we care most about is ourselves just like the animal kingdom.

Death is the end result for both man and animals. Man, though he is a special part of creation, does not escape death. The end of life comes to all of God's creatures. Death and (dust) await both man and beast, regardless of the length or quality of life. What happens next is much a mystery. Even simple questions are relegated to the corners of our minds to be answered at our own passing: Do all dogs really go to heaven?

At the end of a person's life God brings judgment and the judgment of God on a person is hidden from those who are still alive. We are left to wonder about a particular person's eternal state.

22 So I saw that there is nothing better for a person than to enjoy their work, because that is their lot. For who can bring them to see what will happen after them?

Because there are so many unanswerable questions regarding the eternal state of a person, it is not necessary to spend all our lives speculating and wondering about it. We have what we have here and now. It is best to leave the future up to God and go about the tasks that are before us.

ECCLESIASTES 4

¹Again I looked and saw all the oppression that was taking place under the sun:

I saw the tears of the oppressed and they have no comforter; power was on the side of their oppressors and they have no comforter. ² And I declared that the dead, who had already died, are happier than the living, who are still alive. ³ But better than both is the one who has never been born, who has not seen the evil that is done under the sun. ⁴ And I saw that all toil and all achievement spring from one person's envy of another. This too is meaningless, a chasing after the wind.

Sin is the common denominator linking us all. And with it comes oppression. Solomon witnessed those in power oppressing those who are not. Bullying knows no age limit. Those in power take advantage right to the end and no one comes to the aid of the weak. It's sad and it's frustrating, but it is the way life will go when sinful men have the chance to be in power.

The 19th century British politician Lord Acton was speaking the truth when he said, "Absolute power corrupts absolutely." Because sin is in every heart, the only respite from this world full of sinful men is death. Solomon understood that a level above death is not to have been born in the first place. It is the only escape from experiencing and witnessing the sinful actions of mankind. There is no end to the depravity of man:

- In 2008, near Winnepeg Canada, Will Baker stabbed a man several times and then removed his head.
- In 2019 on the outskirts of Hyderabad, India a veterinarian woman was raped by four men. She was then suffocated, and her body was burned and thrown beneath a bridge.
- In 2016 in North Carolina an 11-year-old boy with cuts and bruises and a broken wrist was chained to the front porch, with a dead chicken tied around his neck. The boy was a foster child and was being punished for killing a chicken.
- In 2014 in a fit of anger, nineteen year-old Alan Hruby killed both his parents and his sister.
- In 1998, in Chicago, two boys ages seven and eight kill an eleven year old girl in order to steal her bike.
- 2020, in New Jersey, a lawyer dressed in delivery clothes, shot the husband and son of a judge in their home.

The list seems endless and brings pain on the deepest level. Imagine the pain God feels as he witnesses sin unleashed among his creation.

Solomon further states that the general motivation for achievement is envy. When one sees that another has more, he hungers for more. This drives him toward achievement and becomes his dominating motivation.

> [5] *Fools fold their hands and ruin themselves.* [6] *Better one handful with tranquillity than two handfuls with toil and chasing after the wind.*
>
> [7] *Again I saw something meaningless under the sun:*
>
> [8] *There was a man all alone; he had neither son nor brother. There was no end to his toil, yet his eyes were not content with his wealth. "For whom am I toiling,"* *he asked, "and why am I depriving myself of enjoyment?" This too is meaningless— a miserable business!*

Once again, the King is calling for balance. To do no work, leads to poverty and ruin. We are to work, but not chase work to the point where that is all we do. There will always be more to do and more to acquire. When we have determined how much is enough, it is time to enjoy the tranquility it brings.

Simply put, if you do nothing, you get nothing. Laziness is a foolish way to live. However, if you do nothing but work, you amass plenty, but do not have the time or energy to enjoy it.

Solomon draws us to an example of a man who had plenty to live on but nothing to live for. He was childless and friendless. His eyes continually saw more of what he didn't have. Even in the abundance of things, he was not content. This led to great confusion over his life.

A similar scenario happened in the life of John. John worked his entire life, sacrificed his wife and children on the altar of achievement, and retired a millionaire. He had plenty of stuff, but no one interested in enjoying it with him. Shortly after retiring he was afflicted with Alzheimer's disease and soon didn't even know his own name. He died with plenty in the bank but nothing in his heart. He had spent his entire life building monuments but not memories.

> *9 Two are better than one, because they have a good return for their labor: 10 If either of them falls down, one can help the other up. But pity anyone who falls and has no one to help them up. 11 Also, if two lie down together, they will keep warm. But how can one keep warm alone? 12 Though one may be overpowered, two can defend themselves. A cord of three strands is not quickly broken.*

We are interactive social beings. We are meant to live with each other in harmony and mutual cooperation. During the creation account, God created the entire universe. After he completed a particular aspect of creation, he labeled it "Good." When the task of creation was complete, He labeled it all "Very good."

But in Bible Genesis 2:1, we find the first negative statement in all of history. God states, "It is not good for man to be alone…" With all that is very good, God sees that there is one particular aspect of the man's life that is not good. And that is for the man to be alone.

We are meant to live symbiotically. That means that we need each other, and we need to be needed by each other. This symbiotic relationship is seen in the relationship between a tick bird and a hippopotamus. If you have ever seen a picture of a hippo with a bird on its back, you've witnessed this relationship. The bird on the back of the hippo is a tick bird. It is built with a long beak and lives off the ticks that it digs out from between the folds in the hippo's back. If enough ticks are left unchecked they can take down a good-sized hippo. The way this symbiotic relationship works is this: The hippo provides the ticks that the tick bird eats, and the tick bird alleviates the health issues the ticks cause in the hippo's life.

When we work and live in harmony with one another we find protection, encouragement, progress, and success.

This is where King Solomon shares a set of laws regarding our togetherness:

> *⁹Two are better than one, because they have a good return for their labor.*

The Law of Synergy: The total is better than the sum of the parts.

We see this law on display in the amount of weight two horses can pull. Two horses can pull about nine thousand pounds, but through the power created by adding more horses, four horses can pull over thirty thousand pounds. This is the essence of synergy. In his classic economics text, *The Wealth of Nations*, Adam Smith wrote than ten people working individually can produce twenty pins a day, but ten people working together can produce forty-eight thousand pins a day. It is through a relationship with others that our impact is multiplied.

One day a salesman was driving through the country and lost control of his car skidding into a ditch. He couldn't get his car out. He tried pushing, he tried pulling but there was no way he could move his vehicle. A farmer came along and said, "Can I help you?" The man said, "Yes, I'm stuck in this ditch and I can't get out. Is there any way you could help me get out?" He said, "I don't know if I can help you. The only thing I have is my old, blind mule Dusty. But we'll hook a rope up to your car and we'll get old Dusty to start pullin' and we'll see if we can get you out."

When they got Dusty hooked up to the car, the farmer said, "Come on Skipper let's go!" And he cracked his whip. Then he took his whip again and he cracked it and said, "Come on Festus, let's go!" And he cracked his whip again and hit Dusty and said, "Come on Dusty let's go!" And Dusty started pulling and pulling and he pulled that car right out of the ditch. Then the salesman said, "I really appreciate you getting me out of that ditch but I don't understand something. You have this blind mule all by himself named Dusty. Why in the world did you call out Skipper and Festus and crack the whip the then strike Dusty and get him to pull?" And the farmer said, "Well it's easy. If Dusty thought he was working all by himself he'd know he could never pull this car out of the ditch."

You and I really do need each other!

> ***10 If either of them falls down, one can help the other up. But pity anyone who falls and has no one to help them up.***

The Law of Support: Whether we fall down physically or emotionally, we all need a hand up from time to time. That's one of the reasons friendship really is so important.

In 1953, during the month of May, two men became the first in history to climb to the top of Mt. Everest: Edmund Hillary, a New Zealand beekeeper and explorer, and his Sherpa guide from Nepal, Tenzing Norgay. They reached the summit together and attained instant international fame.

On the way down from the 29,000-foot peak, Hillary slipped and started to fall. He would almost certainly have fallen to his death, but Tenzing Norgay immediately dug in his ice-axe and braced the rope linking them together, saving Hillary's life.

At the bottom the international press made a huge fuss over the Sherpa guide's heroic action. Through it all Tenzing Norgay remained very calm, very professional, and very un-carried away by it all. To all the shouted questions he had one simple answer: "Mountain climbers always help each other." This is the law of support in action.

In his book *Stories for the Heart*, Tim Hansel shares a wonderful story that so illustrates this point. Jimmy Durante was one of the greatest entertainers of a generation ago. He was asked to be a part of a show for World War II veterans. He told them his schedule was very busy and he could afford only a few minutes, but if they wouldn't mind his doing one short monologue and immediately leaving for his next appointment, he would come. Of course, the show's director agreed happily.

But when Jimmy got on stage, something interesting happened. He went through the short monologue and then stayed. The applause grew louder and louder and he kept staying. Pretty soon, he had been on fifteen, twenty, then thirty minutes. Finally, he took a last bow and left the stage. Backstage someone stopped him and said, "I thought you had to go after a few minutes. What happened?"

Jimmy answered, "I did have to go, but I can show you the reason I stayed. You can see for yourself if you'll look on the front row." In the front row were two men, each of whom had lost an arm in the war. One had lost his right arm and the other had lost his left. Together, they were able to clap, and that's exactly what they were doing, loudly and cheerfully. Again, we see the law of support in human form.

> ¹¹ *Also, if two lie down together, they will keep warm. But how can one keep warm alone?*

The Law of Survival: Due to prolonged exposure to extreme cold, hypothermia may set in. This is the inability of a person's body to produce enough heat to sustain life. If left unaddressed death will ensue. Because the person's body cannot create the necessary heat, it is imperative that heat be provided from an outside source. But if the heat from a machine or fire is not available the heat from another's body is needed. In this case, it is imperative that another person get inside a blanket or sleeping bag with the victim. The healthy person's body becomes the source of heat for the one struggling.

> ¹² *Though one may be overpowered, two can defend themselves.*

The Law of Safety: There really is safety in numbers. The advice when facing an aggressive bear in the wild is: 1-Stay together. 2-Don't run. 3-Present yourselves as a united force. 4-Make yourselves appear to be a big as possible. 5-Make as much noise as possible. Being together gives you the greatest chance of surviving an attack.

The law of safety was also illustrated in the manufacturing of parachutes during World War II. At that time, parachutes were being constructed by the thousands. From the workers' point of view, the job was tedious. It involved crouching over a sewing machine eight to ten hours a day and stitching endless lengths of colorless fabric. The result was a formless heap of cloth. But every morning the workers were told that each stitch was part of a life-saving operation.

They were asked to imagine as they sewed, that each parachute might be the one worn by their husbands, their brothers, or their sons. Although the work was hard and the hours long, the women and men on the home front understood their contribution to the larger picture.

The summation of what King Solomon is saying is this: Being together is better than being alone. Alone we are weak but together we are strong. A small stick takes little effort to snap. But several sticks joined together become unbreakable.

Nature gives us many examples of the strength that is found in togetherness. One of these involves geese in flight.

What science has learned from Geese flying in a "V" formation:

- As each bird flaps its wings, it creates an "Uplift" for the bird immediately following. By flying in a "V" formation, the whole flock has at least 71% greater flying range than if each bird flew on it's own. Fact: When a goose flies out of formation, it suddenly feels the drag and resistance of trying to go it alone. It quickly gets back into formation to take advantage of the lifting power of the bird in front of it.
- When the lead goose gets tired, it rotates back into the formation, and another goose flies to the point position.
- The geese flying in formation honk from behind to encourage those up front to keep up their speed.
- When a goose gets sick, wounded, or shot down, two follow it down to lend help and protection. They stay with the fallen goose until it dies or is able to fly again. Then, they launch

out on their own, or fly with another formation to catch up with their flock.

Living life with others truly is better than being alone.

¹³ Better a poor but wise youth than an old but foolish king who no longer knows how to heed a warning. ¹⁴The youth may have come from prison to the kingship, or he may have been born in poverty within his kingdom. ¹⁵I saw that all who lived and walked under the sun followed the youth, the king's successor. ¹⁶ There was no end to all the people who were before them. But those who came later were not pleased with the successor. This too is meaningless, a chasing after the wind.

Solomon is commenting on a personal observation. He is making a statement of extremes. A poor but wise youth compared to a wealthy foolish old king. The youth may have been impoverished due to imprisonment, or he may have been born poor. Poverty and prison can be excellent instructors. It is not explained how the youth rose to power.

Experience and position are not synonymous with wisdom. You are better to follow someone without a position or experience who is wise than a person with experience and position who fails to act wisely.

Solomon's personal observation is that a youth rose to the kingship. So many people followed the youth. He had energy. He had charisma. He was willing to listen to others and he was extremely popular. Both kings mentioned came from a long line of kings and examples of good and bad kings were numerous. But the people who served those kings were not pleased with the way the youth governed. It is not enough to be popular, energetic, and engaging. You must also be wise to be a good leader!

Age is an aid to wisdom and the ability to lead. In Hebrew history thirty-nine kings reigned between Israel and Judah. It is very surprising to note the age of some of those who reigned. Jehoash age 7, Azariah age 16, Manasseh age 12, Josiah age 8, Jehoiachin age

18. It causes one to wonder how those so young could ever inspire hope regarding their ability to lead.

King Solomon didn't live to see this observation take place in his own family, but 1 Kings 12:6-11 tells a story similar to what he relates to us.

After King Solomon died, his son Rehoboam was set to take over the throne. He was in Shechem for his inauguration. The people came to him stating that King Solomon had been hard on them and requesting that he be more lenient. They promised allegiance to him if he granted their request. Rehoboam told them to depart from him for three days while he considered their request.

> *Rehoboam consulted with the elders who had served his father Solomon while he was still alive, saying, "How do you counsel me to answer this people?" ⁷ Then they spoke to him, saying, "If you will be a servant to this people today, and will serve them and grant them their petition, and speak good words to them, then they will be your servants forever." ⁸ But he forsook the counsel of the elders which they had given him, and consulted with the young men who grew up with him and served him. ⁹So he said to them, "What counsel do you give that we may answer this people who have spoken to me, saying, 'Lighten the yoke which your father put on us'?" ¹⁰ The young men who grew up with him spoke to him, saying, "Thus you shall say to this people who spoke to you, saying, 'Your father made our yoke heavy, now you make it lighter for us!' But you shall speak to them, 'My little finger is thicker than my father's loins! ¹¹ Whereas my father loaded you with a heavy yoke, I will add to your yoke; my father disciplined you with whips, but I will discipline you with scorpions.'"*

Rehoboam was forty-one when he became King (1 Kings 14:21). It is likely he was very popular. However, he refused to listen to those with experience and wisdom, instead listening to the young men he ran with. His decision to listen to his buddies led to disaster.

When the people heard his response, they departed and made

Jeroboam their king and the kingdom was divided from that point on.

And so it goes, when a person without wisdom coming with age and experience assumes the lead.

ECCLESIASTES 5

¹Guard your steps when you go to the house of God. Go near to listen rather than to offer the sacrifice of fools, who do not know that they do wrong. ² Do not be quick with your mouth, do not be hasty in your heart to utter anything before God. God is in heaven and you are on earth so, let your words be few.

Going before God is serious business. William Temple has so aptly stated that the definition of worship is: "To quicken the conscience by the holiness of God, to feed the mind with the truth of God, to purge the imagination by the beauty of God, to open up the heart to the love of God, to devote the will to the purpose of God."

Chuck Swindoll notes, "We are often so caught up in our activities that we tend to worship our work, work at our play, and play at our worship.

It is much too common that we go to God with our *Grocery List*. We talk more than we listen and enter with open hands instead of an open heart.

In James 1:19, we find this instruction, "*This* you know, my beloved brethren. But everyone must be quick to hear, slow to speak *and* slow to anger;" Although James is addressing interpersonal relationships this can easily be applied to our time in worship. We are told in Psalm 46:10, "Be still and know that I am God!"

King Solomon admonishes us to think deeply before we speak to God. We are not to engage the Lord lightheartedly or without reverence.

Tom was a college student engaged as a leader in a Christian camp. During the training time with the other leaders he was asked to start the day by leading in prayer before the group. Possibly in an effort to impress the other leaders with the closeness he had with the Almighty, he began his prayer by saying, "Good morning Lord! How's it goin' big fella?" The lack of reverence was evident. Thankfully, a staff member gently and privately addressed this with Tom.

Though we are called to an intimate relationship with God, even calling Him "Abba" (an intimate address), there is no room for flippancy regarding our relationship with the creator of the universe.

> *³ A dream comes when there are many cares, and many words mark the speech of a fool.*

Solomon is speaking of two different fronts. Many cares and many words. It is possible he is thinking of the same person. He mentions two different problems. A person with many cares dreams of relief. Those who listen to his incessant words also dream of relief.

Those who are weighed down with a multitude of cares spend their time dreaming of ways to rid themselves of their burdens. They are not involved with action, only dreams. And when they can't stop talking about their cares, those around them see them as foolish. When problems are only thought about and talked about, foolishness is the appropriate label.

Ivan was a youth minister in a large church. He was very active with the youth and had many plans to help them with the many problems they were encountering. Every time some form of difficulty swept through the youth group, Ivan came up with an event that would address it. The issue was not in the development of plans to combat the issues at hand, the problem was that all he did was talk about it. He never initiated any of his plans. This eventually led to his dismissal. It is not enough to engage in the cares of others, we must go past the talking stage and move into action.

> *⁴ When you make a vow to God, do not delay to fulfill it. He has no pleasure in fools; fulfill your vow. ⁵ It is better not to make a vow than to make one and not fulfill it. ⁶ Do not let your mouth lead you into sin. And*

do not protest to the temple messenger, "My vow was a mistake." Why should God be angry at what you say and destroy the work of your hands? ⁷ Much dreaming and many words are meaningless. Therefore fear God.

Solomon returns to the idea of worship and deals with the issue of making a vow. An agreement lasts until one of the parties is not pleased. Promises are only as good as long as it's convenient. Contracts last only until they reach a deadline. But a vow is the highest form of promise. Vows remain in place until they are completely fulfilled or one of the parties dies. When couples stand before the wedding altar, they often state traditional wedding vows. Most traditional vows end with "until death do us part." In simpler terms, "I will keep these promises until I die."

Before kings were chosen, Israel was led by judges. Those chosen served in both a legal as well as a military position. In Judges 11-12, we learn of Jephthah, Israel's ninth judge who served for six years. During a time when the people of Gilead were oppressed by the sons of Ammon, they summoned Jephthah to lead them. As Jephthah was about to engage in battle with the Ammonites, he made a foolish vow to the Lord. He said, "If you will indeed give the sons of Ammon into my hand, then it shall be that whatever comes out of the doors of my house to meet me when I return in peace from the sons of Amon it shall be the Lord's and, I will offer it up as a burnt offering."

Unfortunately, the first to exit Jephthah's tent was his daughter, his only child. The Bible tells us that Jephthah followed through with his promise and offered up his daughter. Whether or not this was done literally or figuratively is a point of speculation. But Jephthah learned the seriousness of making a foolish vow to the Lord and Solomon warns us against following his example.

Because a vow to God carries such weight and requires a deep level of commitment, Solomon encourages us not to delay in fulfilling it. As time goes by and the difficulty of the vow is engaged, the tendency is to let the vow slip and not fulfill it.

College students see the reality of this in the requirements of individual classes. When the syllabus is handed out, they review what is needed to fulfill the instructor's demands. Many times, this involves a research paper. But too often, students find themselves in panic mode as they reach the end of the semester having ignored the paper. Their delay in fulfilling this requirement leads to much anxiety.

What we say matters to God. When you make a vow to God, pay it immediately. Do not make *off-the-cuff* promises to God. "God, If you get me out of this I will..."

Don't be foolish in making a promise to God, Think it through!

Do not sin with your mouth and cover it by saying it was a mistake. A mistake and a sin are not the same thing!

An unfulfilled promise to God is a sin, and sin carries with it punishment. Don't ask for trouble by making flippant vows.

A relationship with the Lord is serious business. What we say and what we do carry great weight. But mere words and dreaming do not get us anywhere and are a waste of time.

Verse seven is a "bottom line" verse. The King says that in light of all of this we are to "fear" God. This means that we are to honor and revere Him in all things. This includes both what we say as well as our actions.

> *⁸ If you see the poor oppressed in a district, and justice and rights denied, do not be surprised at such things; for one official is eyed by a higher one, and over them both are others higher still. ⁹ The increase from the land is taken by all; the king himself profits from the fields.*

In the late 1960's and early 1970's graft was running wild in the New York Police department. It was difficult to find a police officer who was not in on *the take*. This went from the man walking the beat, all the way up through the entire chain of command. Money was taken in exchange for protection. Eyes looked the other way when injustices were done and crimes were committed. Finally, one man (Frank Serpico) stepped forward and was willing to testify. His action cost him his career in law enforcement and came close to costing him his life. It was found that the corruption was so deep that it took months to sort out once the investigations were underway and many lives were endangered during the process.

Accusations of corruption have recently risen to the surface when the issue of college admission was addressed. Those who had the means were accused of bribing members of the college admittance department by giving large *gifts* to the school.

Whether it's a police force, military organization, sports team, or university, you will not struggle to find points of oppression and corruption. This is part of the fallen nature of man and comes as no surprise.

Because sin resides in the very heart of every man, don't be surprised when you see rampant oppression and a lack of justice. Man does what man is. Even though you go up or down the ladder of authority, you will see oppression and injustice at every level. Every person at each social level takes a piece of *the pie*. Even the one at the highest level (a king), takes a piece of the profits from the fields that others have worked.

> *¹⁰ Whoever loves money never has enough; whoever loves wealth is never satisfied with their income. This too is meaningless. ¹¹ As goods increase, so do those who consume them. And what benefit are they to the owners except to feast their eyes on them? ¹²The sleep of a laborer is sweet, whether they eat little or much, but as for the rich, their abundance permits them no sleep.*

The joy of having money is short-lived. The fact is, money will not bring ultimate satisfaction. There will always be more to be had.

In their newsletter, *Connections*, The Chronicle of Higher Education cited this encounter:

> *Kurt Vonnegut Jr. was invited to a lavish party thrown by a multimillionaire on his estate on Long Island. At the party, Vonnegut ran into a friend, Joseph Heller, author of the novel Catch 22.*
>
> *"Joe," Vonnegut asked, "How does it make you feel to realize that only yesterday our host probably made more money than Catch 22 - one of the most popular books of all time - has grossed worldwide over the past 40 years?"*
>
> *Heller replied, "I have something he can never have."*

"What's that, Joe?"
"The knowledge that I've got enough."

A man was talking about the land he had and the additional land he had his eye on. A friend asked him how much land he desired. He said, "I don't want all the property in the world, just what's attached to mine." This man is suffering from the disease: The "Gottahaves," a progressive disease in which the one afflicted hungers, thirsts, and is consumed with the idea of having more of that which he already has.

Those who are very wealthy share a common fear, that of losing what they have. Some of the cheapest and stingiest people you will meet are those who can afford to be generous.

After completing the filming of a full-length movie, the props from the film were all put in a room for the workers to buy at a deeply discounted price. These were lamps, tables, chairs, rugs, dishes, and numerous other items. Moments before the sale room was opened up, a well-known actress could not resist the pull a bargain. She took over the room and bought nearly everything leaving very little for the workers on the set. She needed nothing but felt she had to have the goods that could be gotten so cheaply. Those nearby saw what Solomon so easily labels "Meaningless."

Along with gaining wealth comes the *friends* that are all too eager to help in the spending of it. Proverbs 19:4, is correct, "Wealth adds many friends, but a poor man is separated from his friend."

It is possible for a person's possessions to increase beyond their ability to enjoy them. The best they will be able to do is to simply stare at all they have. It is reported that comedian Jay Leno's car collection exceeds 150 individual cars. This number, however, is exceeded by Sultan Hassanal Bolkiah of Brunei who owns over 5,000 cars.

A good and honest day of hard work is generally rewarded by a good night's sleep even when there has been little to eat. The headwaters of peaceful sleep are found in the mind, not the stomach. But the one who has abundance is in danger of over-doing it which will keep him from sleeping well. Perhaps their mind is filled with ways to spend their wealth or in fear of losing it all. The old adage is very appropriate here, "There are givers and takers. The takers eat well, but the givers sleep well. The key is moderation both in eating and working.

The wisdom we can gain from the animal kingdom is limitless. Birds build their nests, rear their young, and make their annual flights to other climes. But so far as is known, no bird ever tried to build more nests than its neighbors; No fox ever fretted because he had only one hole in the earth in which to hide; No squirrel ever died in anxiety lest he should not lay up enough nuts for two winters instead of one; No dog ever lost sleep over the fact that he did not have enough bones buried in the ground for his declining years. It is very possible for us to place the emphasis upon the wrong things which can become a catalyst for worry and anxiety manifesting itself in a lack of sleep.

> *[13] I have seen a grievous evil under the sun: wealth hoarded to the harm of its owners, [14] or wealth lost through some misfortune, so that when they have children there is nothing left for them to inherit.*

Solomon sees two disturbing extremes: A man hurts himself to get rich. He hoards everything he gets and spends his time, and mental energy reviewing all he has.

In Mark 10:17-22, we find Jesus encountering a man living the first of these two extremes.

> *[17] "As He was setting out on a journey, a man ran up to Him and knelt before Him, and asked Him, "Good Teacher, what shall I do to inherit eternal life?" [18] And Jesus said to him, "Why do you call Me good? No one is good except God alone. [19] You know the commandments, 'Do not murder, Do not commit adultery, Do not steal, Do not bear false witness, Do not defraud, Honor your father and mother.'" [20] And he said to Him, "Teacher, I have kept all these things from my youth up." [21] Looking at him, Jesus felt a love for him and said to him, "One thing you lack: go and sell all you possess and give to the poor, and you will have treasure in heaven; and come, follow Me." [22] But at these words he was saddened, and*

he went away grieving, for he was one who owned much property."

The man's life showed that he was both wealthy and religious. Yet he went away sad. He was sad because Jesus was asking him to separate himself from his money and follow Him. The man was obviously deeply conflicted and chose to hold on to the familiar things which he had known and enjoyed. The wealth he was hoarding brought harm to his soul.

Daniel Dancer, an English miser, died on September 30, 1794, ending one of the most miserable existences ever recorded. He was a third-generation miser and he followed well the example set by his father and grandfather. Though he had a large tract of land and a substantial annual income, he ate one meal a day. He slept in a sack and his clothes were rags and straw. Once a year he bought a secondhand shirt. If he was offered a pinch of snuff, he accepted and put it in a box. When the box was full, he traded it for candles. If he did not get enough candles that way, he sat in the dark. He was so terrified of being robbed that he dug a mantrap outside his front door and barricaded himself in the house. He came and went through the upper story by means of a ladder which he pulled up when he went in. He was always trying to find obscure places to hide his money. Sometimes he hid it under piles of barnyard manure, giving new meaning to the term "filthy lucre." In 1766 his sister, who worked as his housekeeper, was dying. He refused to call a doctor, saying, "Why should I waste my money in wickedly endeavoring to counteract the will of providence? If the old girl's time is come, the nostrums of all the quacks in Christendom cannot save her now as at any future period." He was living truth of the biblical maxim, "For whoever wants to save his life will lose it" (Matthew 16:25).

The other extreme is the man who makes some poor investments or in some other way loses his wealth leaving nothing for his family. Having money or losing money can be equally damaging.

King Solomon further emphasizes this in Proverbs 13:22, "A good man leaves an inheritance to his children's children, And the wealth of the sinner is stored up for the righteous."

¹⁵ Everyone comes naked from their mother's womb, and as everyone comes, so they depart. They take nothing from their toil that they can carry in their hands.
¹⁶ This too is a grievous evil: As everyone comes, so they depart, and what do they gain, since they toil for the wind? ¹⁷All their days they eat in darkness, with great frustration, affliction and anger.

R. C. Sproul observed that "Life is lived between two hospitals." That is to say that we came possessing nothing including power, and we leave the same way.

This section of Solomon's thinking if revealed in a well-known meeting at Edgewater beach in Chicago in 1923. Attending the meeting were nine of the world's most successful businessmen who gathered to talk about plans for the future and where their investments were going. The meeting included:

- The president of the world's largest independent steel company
- The president of the world's largest utility company
- The president of the world's largest gas company
- The greatest wheat speculator in the world
- The president of the NY stock exchange
- A member of the United States President's cabinet
- The world's most successful speculator on Wall Street
- The head of the world's greatest monopoly
- The President of the bank of international settlements

Just a few years later however, after the stock market crash of 1929 and the great depression that followed, the plight of each of these men was revealed:

- Charles Schwab-President of the world's largest independent steel company: Lived on borrowed money for five years and died bankrupt.
- Samuel Insul-President of the world's largest utility compa-

ny: Died penniless in a foreign country a fugitive from justice.
- Howard Hudson-president of the world's largest gas company: Had gone insane.
- Richard Whitley-president of the NY stock exchange: Was released from Sing-Sing penitentiary.
- Arthur Cutten-the greatest wheat speculator: Died broke.
- Albert Fall-Former member of the President's cabinet: Had been pardoned from prison so that he could die at home.
- Jesse Livermore-Most successful speculator on Wall Street: Committed suicide.
- Ivan Krueger-Head of the world's largest monopoly: Committed suicide.
- Leon Frazier-President of the bank of international settlements: Committed suicide.

These men, who were masters of the financial world, found that their finances had mastered them! They came with nothing and left this life the same way.

The fact is, you came into this world with nothing, and you will leave the same way. It was true then and it is true today, you can't take it with you.

This is humorously seen in the interchange between a wealthy yet greedy man and his wife. The man was told that he had very little time to live and should get his house in order. He told his wife, "They say you can't take it with you, but I don't believe that. At my funeral, I want you to take half of my money and put it in the coffin with me. You can keep the other half."

Shortly thereafter, the man passed away. After the funeral, the woman's friend approached her and asked, "You didn't really do that thing about putting in half the money in his coffin did you? The woman replied, "Of course I did! Didn't you see me drop in the check?"

One day a man was visited by an angel. The angel said, "What can I do for you?" The man said, "Show me the Wall Street Journal one year from today. This way, I will know where to invest and will become a multimillionaire." The angel snapped his fingers and out came a Wall Street Journal marked one year in advance of the date when they were talking. The man flipped the pages of the newspaper, studying the listings and observing which stocks would be high and which ones would be low. But in the midst of his joy, a frown came upon his face and tears began to roll down his eyes because when he looked over on the next page, he saw his face. His picture was in the paper under the obituary column.

Though intrinsically, man knows that the things of life and life itself are temporary, yet he has an insatiable hunger for more. Without the understanding that "You can't take it with you," the desire for more will have a tendency to take over one's life and be the motivating force behind your actions. A lack of clear understanding and acceptance of this *darkness*, breeds frustration, difficulty, and anger and these can become the hallmarks of peoples' lives.

18 This is what I have observed to be good: that it is appropriate for a person to eat, to drink and to find satisfaction in their toilsome labor under the sun during the few days of life God has given them—for this is their lot. 19 Moreover, when God gives someone wealth and possessions, and the ability to enjoy them, to accept their lot and be happy in their toil—this is a gift of God. 20 They seldom reflect on the regrets of their life, because God keeps them occupied with gladness of heart.

The proper perspective is to eat and drink and work hard enjoying what you do. If God's hand of provision opens to you and you receive wealth, enjoy it and be thankful to God for it. Those who see clearly the blessings of life, do this and do not harp on the difficulties that come their way. They are too busy enjoying the good things and have found a way to enjoy themselves on the deepest of levels.

This attitude was evident in the life of an elevator operator. One Monday morning, in a full elevator, the man running the elevator began humming a tune. One passenger, irritated by the man's mood, snapped, "What are you so happy about?" "Well sir," replied the operator happily, "I ain't never lived this day before."

A proper perspective regarding life will naturally lead to a good attitude. It is important to note that no matter what type of weather you encounter, it is without a doubt, the best weather in town!

Life has intrinsic difficulties. The call is not to live in denial, but to emphasize the blessings over the struggles.

Ephesians 2:11-13 tells us, "Therefore remember that formerly you, the Gentiles in the flesh, who are called "Uncircumcision" by the so-called "Circumcision," *which is* performed in the flesh by human hands—*[12] remember that you were at that time separate from Christ, excluded from the commonwealth of Israel, and strangers to the covenants of promise, having no hope and without God in the world. [13] But now in Christ Jesus you who formerly were far off have been brought near by the blood of Christ.*"

As followers of Christ, we can dwell on the past and remember that as sinners we were: Separate from Christ, excluded from the commonwealth of Israel, strangers to the covenants of promise, having no hope, and without God.

And with these descriptive words it is easy to develop a downcast spirit. However, we have the option to acknowledge how God intervened and we are now His children due to the "Blood of Christ." Our spirits can be lifted and our outlook changed when we see how God "Buts in." "But now..." Our condition has changed. Yes we were far off, but now we have been brought near by the blood of Christ! This can change our downcast spirit to and uplifted heart.

ECCLESIASTES 6

¹ I have seen another evil under the sun, and it weighs heavily on mankind: ² God gives some people wealth, possessions and honor, so that they lack nothing their hearts desire, but God does not grant them the ability to enjoy them, and strangers enjoy them instead. This is meaningless, a grievous evil.

³ A man may have a hundred children and live many years; yet no matter how long he lives, if he cannot enjoy his prosperity and does not receive proper burial, I say that a stillborn child is better off than he. ⁴ It comes without meaning, it departs in darkness, and in darkness its name is shrouded. ⁵ Though it never saw the sun or knew anything, it has more rest than does that man— ⁶ even if he lives a thousand years twice over but fails to enjoy his prosperity. Do not all go to the same place?

King Solomon sites a difficulty that is not uncommon but very hard to understand. There are those who are deeply blessed by God. They have money, they have material wealth, and they have popularity. They have no unmet needs or desires. Yet they don't have one thing that money and honor can't buy. For some unexplained reason, they don't have the ability to enjoy all they have. It may be due to declining health or mental difficulties, but the scenario given is not beyond the imagination.

In Daniel 4:28-33, we see what Solomon was talking about. Nebuchadnezzar had it all. As king of Babylon he possessed money, material goods, and honor. Yet in an instant, all that was taken away.

> [28] *All this happened to Nebuchadnezzar the king.* [29]*Twelve months later he was walking on the roof of the royal palace of Babylon.* [30] *The king reflected and said, 'Is this not Babylon the great, which I myself have built as a royal residence by the might of my power and for the glory of my majesty?'* [31] *While the word was in the king's mouth, a voice came from heaven, saying, 'King Nebuchadnezzar, to you it is declared: sovereignty has been removed from you,* [32] *and you will be driven away from mankind, and your dwelling place will be with the beasts of the field. You will be given grass to eat like cattle, and seven periods of time will pass over you until you recognize that the Most High is ruler over the realm of mankind and bestows it on whomever He wishes.'* [33] *Immediately the word concerning Nebuchadnezzar was fulfilled; and he was driven away from mankind and began eating grass like cattle, and his body was drenched with the dew of heaven until his hair had grown like eagles' feathers and his nails like birds' claws.*

At one point in time Stephen Hawking was said to be the most intelligent man in the world. He became famous for his work in both science and mathematics and his discoveries and theories have opened up many insights regarding our universe. He earned over twenty national and international awards including the Albert Einstein Award as well as the Foreign Associate of the National Academy of Sciences. It is estimated that his net worth exceeded $20 million. Wealth, possessions, and honor were securely in the hands of Hawking.

Yet in 1963 he was diagnosed with ALS (Lou Gehrig's Disease) and spent a great deal of the rest of his life physically challenged. His life ended on March 14, 2018 (age 76), with his last days being spent in a wheelchair, unable to talk without a machine, and unable to sit up straight. He is truly an example of a man who had everything except the ability to enjoy it.

It is unnerving to be surrounded by so much, yet not be able to take pleasure in all that is about you.

All of life for every living creature has its end in death. No matter how much one works, worries, and acquires, he still dies with an empty mouth and an open hand. All that you gain physically you will leave behind. Sometimes all our gathering is even enjoyed by someone else. That is out of one's control so there is no point in postulating about it. It IS possible to have plenty to live on and nothing to live for.

> *⁷ Everyone's toil is for their mouth, yet their appetite is never satisfied. ⁸ What advantage have the wise over fools? What do the poor gain by knowing how to conduct themselves before others? ⁹ Better what the eye sees than the roving of the appetite. This too is meaningless, a chasing after the wind.*

Whether we are wise or foolish, we still have a never-ending desire to be fed. No one escapes this need. It is a universal need of both the rich and the poor.

Regarding the poor, Solomon notes that if one learns to act properly but does not know how to get out of poverty, he gains nothing. He is still poor and in the never-ending pursuit of what he doesn't have.

Henry Ford once asked a new manager, "What is your goal?" "Why, to make money, of course!" the man answered. Mr. Ford quietly removed the man's glasses, taped a silver dollar to each lens, put them back on the man's face, and said, "If your goal is to make money then this is all you'll see. Not people. Not God. Not spring flowers. Nor even our fine products. And I pity you."

The pursuit of what you don't have can blind you to all the blessings you do have. The teacher encourages us to enjoy what we possess (what our eye sees) rather than pining away seeking what we lack.

> *¹⁰ Whatever exists has already been named, and what humanity is has been known; no one can contend with someone who is stronger. ¹¹ The more the*

words, the less the meaning, and how does that profit anyone?
[12] For who knows what is good for a person in life, during the few and meaningless days they pass through like a shadow? Who can tell them what will happen under the sun after they are gone?

The King again repeats his feelings on new discoveries. Life goes on whether or not a person is part of it. God has already touched everything so there are no discoveries from His point of view. He is the Almighty and cannot be defeated. Speculating about it changes nothing. You can talk and debate about everything, but mere words change nothing.

The story is told of a man in China who raised horses for a living. When one of his prized stallions ran away, his friends gathered at his home to mourn his great loss. After they had expressed their concern, the man raised this question: "How do I know whether what happened is bad or good?" A couple days later the runaway horse returned with several strays following close behind. The same acquaintances again came to his house-this time to celebrate his good fortune. "But how do I know whether it's good or bad?" the old gentleman asked them. That very afternoon the horse kicked the owner's son and broke the young man's leg. Once more the crowd assembled-now to express their sorrow over the incident. "But how do I know if this is bad or good?" the father asked again. Well, only a few days later, war broke out. The man's son, however, was exempted from military service because of his broken leg.

God who sees the entire picture of the short span of a person's life is the one who decides what is good and what is bad. We are introduced to this in Genesis chapter 1. In the story of creation, it is God who renders the verdict on what He has created at the conclusion of each day. In His judgment, He is the one who labels the creation "Good." When a person's life is over, life and history move on under the hand and plan of God. The man who dies has no control over the life he leaves.

ECCLESIASTES 7

¹A good name is better than fine perfume, and the day of death better than the day of birth.

This is a comment on a person's reputation reflected in his character. Solomon likens a person's name or reputation to perfume. Though perfume gives a small amount of enjoyment, its effects last for only a short time. A person's reputation however is important and will last beyond their lives!

Sir Bartle Frere was once on his way to visit a Scottish home. The master of the household, sending a servant to meet him, sought some description by which the visitor might easily be recognized. He said at last to the servant, "When the train comes in, you will see a tall gentleman helping somebody." The man's reputation truly had preceded him.

How people know and refer to you at the end of your life is more important than at the beginning of your life. Being enamored in the presence of a baby is extremely common. But mourning the loss of life of a great man or woman is of greater value. It speaks of that person living a life of impact and integrity presenting them as a person of character.

Self-evaluation is needed when dealing with the subject of a person's reputation. Is the world a better place because you're in it? Can you name six people who at your funeral will not look at their watch? Will you leave a positive indelible mark on the hearts of those who knew you best? Is your life worth emulating?

This idea is encapsulated in a comment by Sociologist Tony Campolo, "When you were born, you cried and everyone else was happy. I hope that when you die, you'll be happy and everyone else will cry." Your reputation is what will make this concept a reality.

> *² It is better to go to a house of mourning than to go to a house of feasting, for death is the destiny of everyone; the living should take this to heart. ³ Frustration is better than laughter, because a sad face is good for the heart. ⁴ The heart of the wise is in the house of mourning, but the heart of fools is in the house of pleasure.*

This is not a condemnation of life's moments that bring celebration. Rather, it is an admonition to see life as it really is and resist the temptation to think that the world is going to make you happy. Only fools believe that all of life is one big laugh-fest. Reality shows us: Food spoils. People age. Governments collapse. Streams dry up. You must guard against being so optimistic that you set yourself up for continual disappointment. People really do die. It is normal to mourn. Solomon encourages us to take life seriously and live soberly with the end of life in view. When we visit a place where people mourn it gives us a healthy perspective on life. It motivates us to make the adjustments in life that are necessary to bring about a good memory of us after we are gone.

No one enjoys losing. But when you lose you spend time evaluating what went wrong and what corrections you need to make. When you win, you are lost in celebration but do little to change.

For one's heart to be in the house of mourning means to consider one's end. What will it be like when life's breath has left us? What is it that we want others to say regarding our passing? It is in these questions that we measure how to live. There is very little perspective about life that comes about by attending a party.

We are quick to label a commercial good because we enjoy it. If it makes us laugh or sing, we think it is successful. But if we don't remember the product, it is not a good commercial and has not achieved its purpose. And like a good commercial, realizing the finality of life should draw us to the brevity of life.

> *⁵ It is better to heed the rebuke of a wise person than*

to listen to the song of fools. ⁶ Like the crackling of thorns under the pot, so is the laughter of fools. This too is meaningless.

When a wise person corrects you it initially hurts, but it is ultimately good for you. Though the atmosphere around fools is enjoyable... This *party*, ultimately is not good for you.

Jim was a youth minister. At the end of a particular summer, he had planned a "back to school bash" with his youth group. He rented out a local venue, made arrangements for the food, and brought in some out of town entertainment. Everything went well until the end of the evening when the entertainment took the stage. Some of the words they sung were not appropriate for the students to hear. On Monday morning he received a call from one of the parents who were involved. The parent shared with him their concerns in a very mature and amiable way.

Jim had several options to employ regarding his response. He could have said, "You're out of touch!" Or, "This isn't about you. The kids loved it." Or even, "It's my responsibility to decide these things!"

His response resonated with the words of Solomon, "Thanks for telling me that! I appreciate your input."

Sometimes the truth brings about great pain. Sometimes the truth is not easily received. But in the end, truth spoken from a wise and caring person is what brings about the necessary changes in our lives that push us forward.

Solomon likens the laughter of fools to the burning of a thorn bush. The substance of wisdom that you get from fools gives you a little light, a small amount of heat, some noise, and then it's gone. Its influence and benefit go out with the flame. The words from the wise however, may be hurtful at first but when the emotion of the moment fades, the wisdom of their words rises to the top.

⁷ Extortion turns a wise person into a fool, and a bribe corrupts the heart.

Getting money by immoral means turns you into something you may not have intended to become. When you force people to give you money it affects your heart and changes you deep down inside.

People don't begin a life of thievery by embezzling large sums of money. It starts out small and grows. A Woman who was the treasurer for the local Parent Teachers Association ran into some difficulty with her personal finances. So she *borrowed* a small amount from the PTA fund with the intention of paying it back. Before long and before she was able to pay it back, she found herself dipping into the fund for another *temporary* fix. Soon the sums she borrowed grew larger and larger. Before long, the entire amount she stole was in the thousands and she was arrested.

In 2009, Bernie Madoff was convicted of stealing over $60 billion from people's retirement. It started small and grew. As of this writing he sits in a prison outside of Raleigh, N.C. He was sentenced to 150 years in prison. He will in fact, die in prison.

The first time you get money by illegal means and don't get punished makes it easier to do it again. This escalates as time goes on. And before long, this illegal activity corrupts a person's heart and this behavior is seen as normal in the mind of the thief.

Over time, a person's heart gets more and more corrupt and his vision of right and wrong becomes irreparably tainted. This is clearly evident in the life of an immigrant named Alphonse during the early 1900's. In New York City Alphonse joined several gangs as a teenager. He climbed higher and higher in gang life and eventually joined "The Five Points Gang." Later, he moved to Chicago to continue his gangster activities. In Chicago he was involved in bribery, extortion, bootlegging, tax evasion, racketeering, assault, and murder. He eventually became listed as "Public enemy number 1". His perspective on his life, "I have spent the best years of my life giving people the lighter pleasures, helping them have a good time, and all I get is abuse, the existence of a hunted man." These are the words of Al Capone, Chicago's most notorious gangster. His mind had shifted to where he saw his criminal activities as normal, even valiant.

> *8 The end of a matter is better than its beginning, and patience is better than pride.*

Completing a task brings a great feeling of accomplishment. And evaluation is better done after the job is completed. Many people can begin well, but it is only at the completion of a project that judgment is made. A runner may have a great start, but the gold medal is given to the one who finishes in the lead.

Pride causes a person to rush ahead because it gives a feeling of invincibility. A prideful person does not take time to weigh all the options or to seek advice. It takes patience however, to wait through a process. But you are better waiting to see how an event turns out than bragging about how it's going to be. A proud person brags about the outcome before it happens. A patient person waits and lets the process take him to the fulfillment of the event.

> *⁹ Do not be quickly provoked in your spirit, for anger resides in the lap of fools.*

You would be hard pressed to come up with the benefits to your life that anger brings. The list of negative results of anger, however, seems endless. Anger has divided friends, ruined relationships, destroyed families, tainted reputations, and ended lives. Anger is one of the emotions that surfaces readily in the lives of fools. Everyone has a choice in what they want to be known by. Don't be known as an angry person. It's too easy for someone to make the short transition and label you a fool.

In James 1:19 we are instructed, "*This* you know, my beloved brethren. But everyone must be quick to hear, slow to speak *and* slow to anger."

You'll find that foolish people reverse the order James has listed. Fools are quick to become angry, always talking, and never seem to listen.

Patience is one of the evidences of the fruit of the Spirit that Paul shares in his letter to the Galatian Christians. A patient person is not quickly provoked in his spirit.

> *¹⁰ Do not say, "Why were the old days better than these?" For it is not wise to ask such questions.*

Most would agree that The *good old days* weren't always good and it does no good to live in the past. We can reflect on the past and learn from the past, but we cannot relive the past. Looking back limits our ability to look forward. When our minds are only on the past it is difficult to focus on the future. The way to move ahead in life is by thinking about where we are rather than where we've been. Remembering your past can be helpful in avoiding repeating mistakes, but becoming stuck in the past will not help in moving forward. There is a reason why our windshields are so much bigger than our rearview mirror. The goal is to glance behind but focus ahead.

Dr. Howard Hendricks has said, "When your memories are more exciting than your dreams, you've begun to die."

The past is the past and it cannot be changed, so it is important that we be able to let it go and move ahead to the future.

> [11] *Wisdom, like an inheritance, is a good thing and benefits those who see the sun.* [12] *Wisdom is a shelter as money is a shelter, but the advantage of knowledge is this: Wisdom preserves those who have it.*

At this point in his address, King Solomon, a man carrying the wisdom gained from experience addresses the issue of wisdom.

When you acquire wisdom, you have gained a very valuable asset. It is similar to receiving a family inheritance. Like money, it offers the benefit of protection. It can serve as a shield against life's difficulties. But wisdom serves a greater purpose than money. Money can only do so much for you. It can make you comfortable, enable you to have various experiences, and even bring a level of happiness. But it doesn't have the ability to preserve your life. Wisdom however will help you make decisions that may very well save your life. Money, when coupled with wisdom can propel your life the way working hard coupled with working smart can accelerate your success.

A particular country town had an elderly man who was known for his wisdom. Many times when a member of the town had a difficult problem, they would make their way up the hill to the home of the wise man.

One day, two mischievious boys decided to test the old man. They found a small bird and carried it to the residence of the man of wisdom. They planned on asking the man if he thought the bird in their hands was alive or dead. If he said, "dead" they would open their hands and let the bird free. If he said the bird was alive, they would crush the baby bird in their hands proving him wrong.

When they approached the wise one, they asked the question, "Is the bird in our hands alive or dead?"

The old fellow paused for a few moments, then looking the boys in the eyes said, "the answer is in your hands!" Wisdom simply flows from those that are wise.

¹³ Consider what God has done: Who can straighten what he has made crooked?

Observe all that God has done both in the creation around you and in you. It is a demonstration of his power and creativity. God is absolutely sovereign over everything in all of creation.

Sovereignty in its simplest form is defined as; Supreme power or authority. That is to say, there is no power above it and no authority beyond it. That is the position God occupies.

Another description of God is that He is immutable. To be immutable is to be unchanging over time or unable to be changed.

Malachi 3:6 says, "For I, the Lord, do not change; therefore you, O sons of Jacob, are not consumed." We are also told in I Samuel 15:29, "Also the Glory of Israel will not lie or change His mind; for He is not a man that He should change His mind."

Years ago, there was a Broadway play titled, "Your Arm's Too Short To Box With God." Though the play was not a call to honor God, the title says it all. Man at his absolute strongest is no match for the strength of Almighty God.

While in second grade, our son shared with his teacher a comment on the sovereignty of God. The previous day a humorous quiz was given over the intercom. The question was presented: "Why do hummingbirds sing?" The answer: "Because they don't know the words." Our son must have mulled over that answer all night. The next day, he pulled aside his teacher and explained, "Hummingbirds don't hum because they don't know the words. They hum because that's the way God made them."

Everything that is done by the movement of the hand of God

functions exactly the way God intended it to. You cannot change God and you cannot change what He does. Your choice lies in your response to all He has done and all He brings your way.

In James Whitcomb Riley's book *Farm Rhymes*, his poem *Wet-Weather Talk* contains these words:

> I hain't no use to grumble and complain:
> It's jest as cheap and easy to rejoice. —
> When God sorts out the weather and sends rain,
> W'y, rain's my choice.

¹⁴ When times are good, be happy; but when times are bad, consider this: God has made the one as well as the other. Therefore, no one can discover anything about their future.

Jesus tells us in Matthew 5:45, "...for He causes His sun to rise on *the* evil and *the* good and sends rain on *the* righteous and *the* unrighteous."

That is to say, God makes good days and bad days. When good days come, enjoy them. When bad days come, use them to learn and grow. You do not know what the next day brings so just evaluate your days as they unfold and live your life knowing that God is in charge.

This is played out in the story of a man struggling for survival. The only survivor of a shipwreck washed up on a small, uninhabited island. He prayed feverishly for God to rescue him, and every day he scanned the horizon for help, but none seemed forthcoming.

Exhausted, he eventually managed to build a little hut out of driftwood to protect him from the elements and to store his few possessions. But then one day, after scavenging for food, he arrived home to find his little hut in flames, the smoke rolling up to the sky, the worst had happened; everything was lost. He was stung with grief and anger. "God, how could you do this to me?" he cried.

Early the next day, however, he was awakened by the sound of a ship that was approaching the island. It had come to rescue him. With both excitement and amazement, he met them on the beach as they came ashore. "How did you know I was here?" asked the weary man of his rescuers. "We saw your smoke signal," they replied.

> **¹⁵ In this meaningless life of mine I have seen both of these: the righteous perishing in their righteousness, and the wicked living long in their wickedness. ¹⁶ Do not be over-righteous, neither be over-wise— why destroy yourself? ¹⁷ Do not be over-wicked, and do not be a fool—why die before your time? ¹⁸ It is good to grasp the one and not let go of the other. Whoever fears God will avoid all extremes.**

King Solomon does some very serious self-evaluation. Within the context of all he has observed he conclude that life doesn't always seem fair. Bad things happen to good people and good things happen to bad people. Likewise, good things happen to good people and bad things happen to bad people. Life carries with it a measure of unpredictability and trying to make complete sense of it and run it through our grid of fairness is a waste of mental energy.

Solomon then admonishes his listeners not to carry their lives to extremes. Don't be misguided into thinking that your righteousness will extend your life. But wickedness and foolishness will have a tendency to shorten your life.

This is humorously demonstrated by the question, "What are the last four words of a fool?" The answer: "Hey guys! Watch this!"

Relax and be yourself. Be comfortable in your own skin. Being overly righteous from an outward perspective can make you judgmental and cause you to take on a "holier than thou" attitude.

Lenny complimented his friend on the jacket he was wearing. He asked him where he got it and was told, "Man, God has been so good to me! He has blessed me in way I could never imagine. We need to let go and rely on His goodness. He really will supply all our needs." My friend just looked down and inwardly shook his head. He told me, "I just wanted to know what store the jacket came from. I wasn't asking for a sermon!"

A group of college students were enjoying a camping trip. They were bedding down for the night in a large tent. Conversation died down and it was time to drift off to get what sleep could be had. As soon as the tent was silent, one of the young men began to recite from memory an entire chapter from the book of revelation. No one asked him to do that! When he finally finished, the tent continued to be silent. It was clear that he was a fellow who felt it was important for the others to know how righteous he was. His demonstration did little to cause the men to hold him in high regard.

After preaching a sermon, Charles Haddon Spurgeon, the great preacher of England was once approached by a woman. She told him that she thought he was egotistical and a braggard. For several minutes she cited his shortcomings and weaknesses. When the proper time came for him to respond, he simply said, "Madam, you've cited my shortcomings, but you don't know the half of it." He was telling her, "I'm a lot worse than you think." He had a proper perspective on his life and pursuit of holy living.

The same can be said about being overly wise. An overly wise person is unapproachable. He's a "know-it-all" kind of person and sees every conversation as an opportunity to give a wisdom revealing lesson. When he can, he will direct the attention of the group his way so he can display his intelligence. True friendships are hard to build when you have the attitude of being the holiest and wisest person in the crowd.

A preacher in a small country church was debating whether or not to hold services one Sunday because of a snowstorm. He decided to go ahead with the service and opened the doors to the church. He was disappointed when only one person, a stranger showed up. He asked the man if he thought it would be wise to go ahead with the sermon he had prepared being that there was only one person there. The man replied, "If I had only one sheep, I would still feed him."

Understanding this, the pastor went ahead with his sermon and preached it as if the church was completely full. In fact, he preached and preached and preached and went way past the time he would normally preach.

When he was finally finished, he asked the man for his thoughts. The man responded, "I told you that if I had one sheep, I would still feed him, but I wouldn't feed him everything I had in the barn."

So often the adage is true, "still waters run deep." It is not necessary to tell everything you know nor to wear your holiness on your sleeve.

¹⁹ Wisdom makes one wise person more powerful than ten rulers in a city.

One person who knows the solution to any problem is better than a room full of people with only authority.

A very important machine had broken down in a manufacturing plant. Several people had been called to fix the machine, but no one could come up with the solution. Then a certain man who showed up. He looked the machine over then hit it with a hammer. To everyone's amazement, the machine started right up. When he handed his bill to the man in charge, the manager was shocked. The bill came to $1,001. "For what?" he asked. The service man replied, "$1.00 to hit the machine with a hammer, and $1,000 to know where to hit it."

The Great Wall of China is the longest man-made structure in the world, with a total length of about 13,170 miles. It was built over the course of hundreds of years by six different dynasties and is over 2,300 years old. And no army has ever conquered China by destroying the wall.

However, in 1214 the massive Mongolian invaders led by Genghis Khan entered and conquered China. But they didn't do it by conquering the wall. They did it by studying the wall, gathering information about the structure and entering through weak points and natural breaches in the wall. It was not by brute strength but by wisdom that China was invaded and victory was attained.

²⁰ Indeed, there is no one on earth who is righteous, no one who does what is right and never sins.

Except for Jesus, there is not one person on earth who has lived their life in right standing with God. Everyone sins! This is innate in a man's soul. It is part of a person's DNA handed down through generations through the line of Adam and Eve.

1 John 1:8 tells us, "If we say that we have no sin, we are deceiving ourselves and the truth is not in us."

In Psalms. 14:3 we find, "They have all turned aside; together they have become corrupt; there is none who does good, not even one.

And in Romans. 3:10-12 the word of God says, "as it is written: "None is righteous, no, not one; no one understands; no one seeks for God. All have turned aside; together they have become worthless; no one does good, not even one."

The word sin is an archery term. It is the distance an arrow lands in relation to the bull's eye. The distance from the bull's eye to the arrow is the *sin mark*. No one (except Jesus Christ) has lived a life without mistakes-without missing the *bull's eye* of moral perfection. This is what Romans 3:23 is addressing when it says, "...for all have sinned and fall short of the glory of God..." King Solomon is simply pointing out what each of us intrinsically knows even if we are reluctant to admit it.

> [21] *Do not pay attention to every word people say, or you may hear your servant cursing you—* [22] *for you know in your heart that many times you yourself have cursed others.*

Words carry great weight. In some cases, they can mean the difference between life and death. The King warns us to be careful about what we hear and what we say. We are to receive all information and speech gently and not take it to heart.

Several years ago, Sales for the Chevy Nova was relatively encouraging for the manufacturers. motivated by U.S. sales, Chevrolet began to market the American Nova throughout the world. Unfortunately, the Nova did not sell well in Mexico and other Latin American countries. Additional ads were ordered and marketing efforts were ramped up, but sales remained stagnant. Sales directors were baffled. The car had sold well in the American market; why wasn't it selling now? When they discovered the answer, it was rather embarrassing: In Spanish, Nova means *No go*.

The business world is full of such stories. For example, when Perdue Farms, Inc., converted its popular slogan "It takes a tough man to make a tender chicken," into Spanish in hopes of expanding its chicken business, the results were less than desirable. Why? The translation was "It takes a virile man to make a chicken affection-ate." Not exactly what Frank Perdue had in mind.

Bear in mind:

- What we hear may not be what is said.
- What they said may not be what is meant.

A humorous look at this was spoken by Alan Greenspan, econo-mist and former chair of the U.S. federal reserve. "I know you think you understand what you thought I said but I'm not sure you realize that what you heard is not what I meant"

This is further illustrated by an episode involving seventeen-year-old Jacob who was getting ready to join his friends waiting for him in the driveway.

As he left the house, he heard his mother ask his father, "Do you like the meatloaf I made?" His father replied, "No I don't like it.

When Jacob got into the car, he told his friends, "Let's go! My parents are about to have a big fight!"

Had he hesitated at the door for a few moments mover he would have heard the conversation in its entirety. The conversation in fact, went this way: Mother: "Do you like the meatloaf I made?" Father: "No, I don't like it. I love it! It's the best meatloaf I've ever had!"

Mother: Thank you dear!"

Father: You are such a good cook!"

This was hardly the blowup Jacob was anticipating. He would have done well to spend some time with King Solomon.

Solomon continues to direct us. Everyone, at one time or anoth-er misspeaks. You have experienced misunderstanding yourself so don't be too quick to put a lot of weight on what is said by others.

23 All this I tested by wisdom and I said, "I am deter-mined to be wise"-but this was beyond me. 24 Whatever exists is far off and most profound-who can discover it? 25 So I turned my mind to understand, to investigate and to search out wisdom and the scheme of things and to understand the stupidity of wickedness and the mad-ness of folly.

Solomon's quest for knowledge never left him. He continued in his pursuit of information and experience. He concluded that to know everything is impossible. Still, he pressed on and he saw that it is foolish to be wicked and worthless to be involved in silly pursuits.

> [26] *I find more bitter than death the woman who is a snare, whose heart is a trap and whose hands are chains. The man who pleases God will escape her, but the sinner she will ensnare.*

There is a type of woman with whom a relationship will be a trap. She will ensnare a man. Both her heart and her hands (body) will capture you and imprison you.

Today, more men (and women) are addicted to pornography than ever before. It is a 13 billion-dollar-a-year industry with over $3,000 spent every second.

Tony was a businessman with several out of town accounts. On his frequent out of town trips to the same city, he began to seek the entertainment in an adult club for men. During these visits he became acquainted with one of the women involved in entertaining and he began to see her and date her. The result of his poor choices caused him to leave his wife and daughter and move in with the woman. Within a year, the woman left him and moved on. Due to child support responsibilities, alimony, and how much the other woman cost him financially, he is left, financially broke, emotionally lonely and living with the residue of being involved with a woman who ensnared his heart and ruined his life.

The answer is to change pursuits. Instead of pursuing pleasure and self-gratification, we must pursue godliness and a right relationship with the Creator. If not, then the relationship a person develops with another may trap his mind, and perhaps his body.

> [27] *Look," says the Teacher, this is what I have discovered: Adding one thing to another to discover the scheme of things.* [28] *While I was still searching but not finding-I found one upright man among a thousand, but not one upright woman among them all.*

Solomon is still trying to piece all of life together and figure out how everything works. He concluded that searching for upright people is futile. It is highly rare to find one! He is not claiming that there are no upright women but is stating that his experience has not brought him into contact with one.

> ²⁹ **This only have I found: God created mankind upright, but they have gone in search of many schemes."**

Babies are born with an air of innocence. But because of their *sin nature* they are also born with, their selfishness comes forth and is displayed in their behavior as they grow. Children are not taught to be selfish. No one has to teach them how to lie or steal. This comes naturally as their sin nature displays itself. No one continues with the apparent life of uprightness.

ECCLESIASTES 8

¹Who is like the wise? Who knows the explanation of things? A person's wisdom brightens their face and changes its hard appearance.

Wisdom allows a man to see the big picture. He doesn't feel the need to move to extremes. And because he knows how things work his face will change and brighten up. Hindsight tends to yield insight.

When you have insight, you have a sense of wealth and control. It's similar to having inside information. People with wisdom tend to delay pushing the panic button. People with wisdom tend to avoid following the crowd. People with wisdom exhibit a sense of peace. And all these attributes can be exhibited on a person's face.

During a trip to Europe to visit family members, Henry arrived just in time to watch a professional soccer game in his cousin's crowded living room watching a soccer game. The mood was loud and nervous with everyone yelling and cheering. Though Henry loved the game and was a big fan of one of the teams, he didn't seem to carry the same nervousness of everyone else in the room.

Henry didn't panic. Henry didn't get emotional. Henry didn't get anxious. All this was due to the fact that Henry had some inside information and was confident his team was going to win. Henry's demeaner was completely based on the fact that he had watched the time-delayed game on the plane while on his way to Europe. He knew the outcome and it displayed itself on his face and in his behavior.

Malcomb was a custodian in an Elementary school. The children all loved him because he was always kind and friendly. One day, as he was exiting the Janitor's closet, a teacher stopped him and asked, "Malcomb, how come you're always in such a great mood?" Malcomb smiled, reached back in the closet and pulled out his Bible. He held the book up and said, "I read the book and know how it ends."

Malcomb's wisdom moved from his head to his heart and migrated to his face.

> *² Obey the king's command, I say, because you took an oath before God. ³ Do not be in a hurry to leave the king's presence. Do not stand up for a bad cause, for he will do whatever he pleases. ⁴ Since a king's word is supreme, who can say to him, "What are you doing?"*
>
> *⁵ Whoever obeys his command will come to no harm, and the wise heart will know the proper time and procedure. ⁶ For there is a proper time and procedure for every matter, though a person may be weighed down by misery.*

Solomon encourages us to obey the rulers over us. They are under an oath of God. We must not abandon our loyalty to them. They are the authority over us. If we obey them, we may side-step a lot of trouble. We can't control a ruler any more than we can control the wind. We also don't know what God will do with and through a ruler. Some rulers are wicked and make evil decisions. But we must remember that ultimately, God is in control. He puts rulers in place, and in His right time, He will take them out.

In Romans 13:1-7 Paul exhorts us in the same direction as King Solomon: Every person is to be in subjection to the governing authorities. For there is no authority except from God, and those which exist are established by God.

> *² Therefore whoever resists authority has opposed the ordinance of God; and they who have opposed will receive condemnation upon themselves. ³ For rulers are not a cause of fear for good behavior, but for evil. Do you want to have no fear of authority? Do what is good,*

and you will have praise from the same; ⁴for it is a min-ister of God to you for good. But if you do what is evil, be afraid; for it does not bear the sword for nothing; for it is a minister of God, an avenger who brings wrath on the one who practices evil. ⁵Therefore it is necessary to be in subjection, not only because of wrath, but also for con-science' sake. ⁶For because of this you also pay taxes, for rulers are servants of God, devoting themselves to this very thing. ⁷Render to all what is due them: tax to whom tax is due; custom to whom custom; fear to whom fear; honor to whom honor.

Pontius Pilot made the decision that led to the death of Christ, but his death led to the opportunity for every man, woman, and child to experience the forgiveness of God and eternity in heaven. After the fateful death of Christ, Pontius Pilot experienced his own death by suffering through the devouring of intestinal worms. His life is proof that God's hand may move slowly, but it moves relent-lessly.

⁷Since no one knows the future, who can tell some-one else what is to come? ⁸As no one has power over the wind to contain it, so no one has power over the time of their death. As no one is discharged in time of war, so wickedness will not release those who practice it. ⁹All this I saw, as I applied my mind to everything done under the sun. There is a time when a man lords it over others to his own hurt.

Solomon tells us emphatically, we *DO NOT* know what tomorrow brings! Those who claim to know the future are only guessing at best. This includes small matters such as the outcome of a contest, as well as large matters such as death. The time of our death is completely in the hands of God. We should not wear ourselves out trying to discern the future and the length of our lives.

Furthermore, wicked people do wicked things and it can bring trouble into their lives. We must bear in mind that God is in charge and He will bring that wickedness back on that person.

In the Hebrew tongue, the word wickeness is *Rasha*. It's connotation is always that of evil or immorality. The root word for this is *Ra*. This In the Hebrew tongue the word wickedness is rendered as *Rash*. The root word means to break. It can be said that a wicked person is one who breaks from the will and commands of God. Going further, we can understand that a person who does evil against another person somehow *Breaks* that other person. If one physically attacks someone, he literally breaks the one he attacks. When the tongue is used to speak evil of someone, their reputation can be broken. This wicked act can cause an untold amount of damage and God will call that wicked person into account.

Chuck Swindoll gives a great example of this in his book *Quest For Character*:

> I read this past week of a couple (let's call them Carl and Clara) whose 25 year marriage was a good one. Not the most idyllic, but a good one. They now had three grown children who loved them dearly. They were also blessed with sufficient financial security to allow them room to dream about a lakeside retirement home. They began looking. A widower we'll call Ben was selling his place. They liked it a lot and returned home to talk and plan. Months passed.
>
> Last fall, right out of the blue, Clara told Carl she wanted to divorce. He went numb. After all these years, why? And how could she deceive him... How could she have been nursing such a scheme while they were looking at a retirement home? She said she hadn't been. Actually, this was a recent decision now that she had found another man. Who? Claire admitted it was Ben, the owner of the lake house, whom she had inadvertently ran into several weeks after they had discussed the sale. They'd begun seeing each other. Since they were now "in love" there was no turning back. Not even the kids, who hated the idea, could dissuade their mother.
>
> On the day she was to leave. Carl walked through the kitchen toward the garage. Realizing she would be gone when he returned, he hesitated, "Well, hon, I guess this

is the last time—" his voice dissolved as he broke into sobs. She felt uneasy, hurriedly got her things together, and drove north to join Ben. Less than two weeks after she moved in with Ben, her new lover, he was seized with a heart attack. He lingered a few hours... and then died.

V. 9 - When a person takes the position of authority over others, it can turn back and bite him as a snake bites its handler. This is depicted in the authority that Uzziah exercised over the Israelites. In 2 Chronicles 26, we read Uzziah's story. He was selected as King by the people of Judah when he was sixteen years old and reigned in Judah for fifty-two years in Jerusalem. For the most part he was a godly King and followed the commands of the Lord. During his reign he became extremely successful and won many battles against the surrounding armies. His military might grew, and he raised an army of over 300,000 warriors. His power and his fame increased as did his wealth. This proved to be his downfall.

> [16] *But when he became strong, his heart was so proud that he acted corruptly, and he was unfaithful to the Lord his God, for he entered the temple of the Lord to burn incense on the altar of incense.* [17] *Then Azariah the priest entered after him and with him eighty priests of the Lord, valiant men.* [18] *They opposed Uzziah the king and said to him, "It is not for you, Uzziah, to burn incense to the Lord, but for the priests, the sons of Aaron who are consecrated to burn incense. Get out of the sanctuary, for you have been unfaithful and will have no honor from the Lord God."* [19] *But Uzziah, with a censer in his hand for burning incense, was enraged; and while he was enraged with the priests, the leprosy broke out on his forehead before the priests in the house of the Lord, beside the altar of incense.* [20] *Azariah the chief priest and all the priests looked at him, and behold, he was leprous on his forehead; and they hurried him out of there, and he himself also hastened to get out because the Lord had smitten him.* [21] *King Uzziah was a leper to the day of his death; and he lived in a separate house, being a leper, for*

he was cut off from the house of the Lord. And Jotham his son was over the king's house judging the people of the land (2 Chronicles 26:16-21).

¹⁰ Then too, I saw the wicked buried—those who used to come and go from the holy place and receive praise in the city where they did this. This too is meaningless.

There are people who are evil (wicked) and still practice religion and garner the respect of their peers. They come and go to the religious centers with notable regularity. Their religious practices however, are in place as a *good luck charm*. It goes no farther in their lives than the exit door of the church.

The difficulty many people have with those who are religious is the fact that their religious activity is confined to the inside walls of the church and only exercised on one day a week. Christians develop this lifestyle by embracing the idea that there is a dual life for the followers of Christ. They hold that there is a *sacred* side and there is a *secular* side to their lives. Going to church, reading their Bible, and participating in other church sponsored activities all fall into the category of the *sacred* side of life. But the workplace, vacations, their home life, and Friday night activities are placed in the *secular* side. This should not be. For the true followers of Christ, there is but one life, and it is all in the sacred category. The world is not fooled by this lifestyle of duplicity and it is one if the reasons why they want nothing to do with the church and those whom attend.

An example of living a life of duplicity is seen in the life of Cerissa Riley. In 2018 she, along with Orthopedic Surgeon Grant Robicheaux, were arrested on charges of drugging, raping and sexually assaulting several women while recording the assaults. She clearly had a secular/sacred paradigm working in her life.

In an interview by several who knew her, she was labeled an Evangelical Christian Missionary and very involved with church activities.

Another example of living a life of duplicity is shown by a man named Dennis. Dennis was heavily involved in church. He served as an usher, attended a Sunday School class, and was a leader in the FAITH evangelism program. He married a woman with whom he attended church, and all seemed to be going well.

However, a year later he was arrested and convicted of burglarizing homes with a woman he was having an affair with.

How can these things be? It comes down to a distinct disconnect between what a person believes and how a person lives.

Orthodoxy means "right belief." Orthopraxy means "right conduct." The further a person's orthodoxy moves from his orthopraxy the more pronounced is his hypocrisy.

People steeped in this disconnect make no lasting positive impressions on those about them. Their names are not revered, and they are not remembered with any lasting honor or respect.

> *11 When the sentence for a crime is not quickly carried out, people's hearts are filled with schemes to do wrong. 12 Although a wicked person who commits a hundred crimes may live a long time, I know that it will go better with those who fear God, who are reverent before him. 13 Yet because the wicked do not fear God, it will not go well with them, and their days will not lengthen like a shadow.*

When lawbreakers are not dealt with quickly, the hearts of those in society are greatly influenced. Some see this as an example to follow, and crime increases because the penalty for doing so is overtaken by the benefits they see in doing wrong.

Times have changed! According to the Bureau of Justice Statistics, the average time spent on death row before execution in 1985 was 71 months — or just less than 6 years. Now, it's eclipsing 20 years. This is disheartening to those who are related to the victims.

Our judicial system is replete with long drawn out court cases filled with loopholes and mismanagement. In many cases, a person given a "Life sentence" is released after fifteen years. Many who are convicted of rape are released after five years.

King Solomon proposes that seeing justice delayed or thwarted brings about a rise in criminal activity and a decline of confidence in the judicial system.

Many do evil because it *appears* that their activity is ignored. BUT God has the final say and He WILL bring about justice. On the outside it appears that the wicked are doing well, but rest assured, God's watchful eyes see every action and He will bring every thought and action under His judgment.

> *14 There is something else meaningless that occurs on earth: the righteous who get what the wicked deserve, and the wicked who get what the righteous deserve. This too, I say, is meaningless. 15 So I commend the enjoyment of life, because there is nothing better for a person under the sun than to eat and drink and be glad. Then joy will accompany them in their toil all the days of the life God has given them under the sun.*

We have a natural tendency to define justice according to our terms. Somehow, we feel equipped to be able to judge how an outcome should be based on our view of fairness. And when things don't turn out the way we feel they should, we cry out against it.

Bad things, however, do happen to good people and good things happen to bad people. Why this happens, we don't know. Positioning ourselves as scorekeepers is meaningless. It is a waste of energy trying to keep God in line so that He can meet our definition of fairness. Solomons view is that it is better that one should work hard and enjoy the benefits of their labor and the good things in life that come.

> *16 When I applied my mind to know wisdom and to observe the labor that is done on earth—people getting no sleep day or night— 17 then I saw all that God has done. No one can comprehend what goes on under the sun. Despite all their efforts to search it out, no one can discover its meaning. Even if the wise claim they know, they cannot really comprehend it.*

The world is so very complex and there is so much to know and discover that no one in an entire lifetime will be able to know or discover it all. The wonders of the world are so deep and vast that no one can stretch his hand to touch them all.

With every discovery we find that there is more to know. Once man had developed the ability to fly, he busied himself with flying faster, farther and longer. Airplanes became rocket ships and a trip across the country developed into trips around the world. Then traveling through the entire world led us into space exploration. As we explore space, we find that there is ore space to explore. Man is involved in a never-ending pursuit to see it all.

ECCLESIASTES 9

¹So, I reflected on all this and concluded that the righteous and the wise and what they do are in God's hands, but no one knows whether love or hate awaits them. ² All share a common destiny-the righteous and the wicked, the good and the bad the clean and the unclean, those who offer sacrifices and those who do not. As it is with the good, so with the sinful; as it is with those who take oaths, so with those who are afraid to take them. ³ This is the evil in everything that happens under the sun: The same destiny overtakes all.

The hearts of people, moreover, are full of evil and there is madness in their hearts while they live, and afterward they join the dead. ⁴ Anyone who is among the living has hope-even a live dog is better off than a dead lion!

⁵ For the living know that they will die, but the dead know nothing; they have no further reward, and even their name is forgotten. ⁶ Their love, their hate and their jealousy have long since vanished; never again will they have a part in anything that happens under the sun.

Solomon stresses that it is the wise person who keeps the end of life in mind. Statistics are that one out of every one person dies. All people good and bad die-it is the fate of all the living. Your behavior good or bad, *still* brings you to the grave. It is wise to understand that ultimately your life, and your death are in the hands of God! The king stresses that our behavior does not absolve us from the final destiny of us all. Righteous or unrighteous living, good or bad behaviour, being clean or not, taking oaths or not, changes nothing. Death is the final veil that will fall on all of us. It is the permanent fate of all the living. This is not desirable and may not seem *fair* but it is the harsh and universal reality of life.

> *⁷ Go, eat your food with gladness, and drink your wine with a joyful heart, for God has already approved what you do. ⁸ Always be clothed in white, and always anoint your head with oil. ⁹ Enjoy life with your wife, whom you love, all the days of this meaningless life that God has given you under the sun—all your meaningless days. For this is your lot in life and in your toilsome labor under the sun.*

King Solomon's recipe is for us not to focus on the fact that life does not go on forever. He suggests we avoid worrying about the day of our death and advises us to simply do what we can-work and play, labor and rest. Life should be enjoyed, and fulfillment should be pursued.

Tim Hansel captures this idea well by saying, "There is no box made by God nor us but that the top can be blown off and the sides flattened out to make a dance floor on which to celebrate life."

When W.E. Sangster learned that he was dying, he made four resolutions:

1. I will never complain.
2. I will keep the home bright.
3. I will count my blessings.
4. I will try to turn it to gain.

Solomon suggests two specific areas while considering the brevity of life: Clothing oneself in white and anointing one's head with oil.

In context biblically, white garments are a symbol of conquest, righteousness, and peace. With this in mind, it appears that Solomon advises us to strive for victory, live righteously, and pursue peace.

Anointing one's head with oil is a symbolic way of setting oneself apart for the service of the Lord. In the old testament, kings were anointed with oil by the prophets to serve as notice that they were chosen by God and are called to serve him in their authoritative positions. Saul (I Sam. 10:1), David (I Sam. 16:13), (I Kings 1:39) and Solomon himself (I Kings 1:39) went through the process of being anointed with oil by prophets signifying God's pleasure in setting them aside to lead His people.

> **¹⁰ Whatever your hand finds to do, do it with all your might, for in the realm of the dead, where you are going, there is neither working nor planning nor knowledge nor wisdom.**

God put work into our lives. He expects us to put life into our work. The short years we have to live are to be lived with purpose and enthusiasm.

Solomon didn't have the Latin words to say, but if he did, he would be calling out, "Carpe Diem!" Seize the day!

Whether at work or at play, the King directs us to be fully committed.

This is illustrated in the story of the pig and the hen. One day a pig and a hen were walking down the road. They came across a billboard that said "Fight world hunger!" The hen turned to the pig and said "We should do something about that!" The pig agreed and asked, "What do you think we should do?" The hen suggested, "Let's host a ham and eggs breakfast!" The pig thought that was a good idea but after thinking about it said, "For you, that's a contribution but for me it's a total commitment."

King Solomon is interested in full commitment. And admonishes us to give it our all.

In Colossians 3:23, Paul carries this same idea, "Whatever you do, do your work as unto the Lord, and not unto men."

Because this life is all we have for the time we have it, the key is to give it our all!

Many ropes courses contain an obscacle called the *Multi-vine* in their high elements area. The multi-vine consists of a tight wire to walk on with a safety wire above it. Hanging vertically from the wire are several ropes. The participant must walk along the wire using the hanging ropes to maintain balance. The problem is that each vertical rope is not long enough to reach the next rope. In order to advance, one must let go of the rope behind him. This requires great focus, concentration, and commitment.

Likewise, in life, in order to move ahead, one must let go of the past, and reach forward to the future. This calls for an *All in* mentality.

> [11] *I have seen something else under the sun:*
> *The race is not to the swift or the battle to the strong, nor does food come to the wise or wealth to the brilliant or favor to the learned; but time and chance happen to them all.*

Time and chance are part of life. Even the smart, gifted, prepared, and wealthy have to take into account time and the unplanned events of life.

- Though the ship was massive and labeled "unsinkable" the Titanic still sunk due to hitting an iceberg.
- Though the power source was extremely complex, on July 13, 1977, New York City was darkened when a bolt of lightning struck a substation.
- Though the greatest of minds worked together to create the spaceship, gaskets that had become brittle due to freezing temperatures allowed fuel to leak and caused the explosion that destroyed the spaceship "Challenger."
- Ed Monaghan was a fighter pilot during World War II. During a "dog-fight" his life was spared due to the enemy's bullet hitting a piece of metal that stood between the bullet and the side of his head.

There are unplanned problems as well as "lucky breaks" that come to all of us no matter our station in life. Our reaction to them is what defines us and reveals our personality and character. The

King is giving credence to the adage: "Expect the unexpected."

> ¹² *Moreover, no one knows when their hour will come: As fish are caught in a cruel net, or birds are taken in a snare, so people are trapped by evil times that fall unexpectedly upon them.*

No one knows the length of his life. No one knows when time and chance will overtake them. Life simply happens and the end of life and difficult times as well as beneficial times do come!

Life is unpredictable. Army Air Force Staff Sgt. Alan Magee can attest to this. On January 3, 1943, his plane was shot by anti-aircraft guns and became a ball of flames. Magee climbed into the fuselage to get his chute and bail out, but it had been shredded by the flak. As Magee was trying to figure out a new plan, a second flak burst tore through the aircraft and then a fighter blasted it with machine gun fire. He was knocked unconscious and blasted from the aircraft at 22,000 feet.

He fell into the town of St. Nazaire and through the glass roof of the train station. He was later found dangling on the steel girders that supported the ceiling.

The glass had slowed his fall and he regained consciousness as German soldiers took him to medical care. Magee's right leg and ankle were broken, he had 28 wounds from shrapnel and glass, and his right arm was cut nearly the whole way off. He had also suffered numerous internal injuries but he lived to tell his story.

Contrastly, 58 year-old Mark John Jollie of Milwaukee, Wis. died simply by slipping on a patch of ice and falling on the pavement injuring his head.

One man falls 22,000 feet and lives. Another man falls less that six feet and dies. No one knows their time.

In Luke 12, Jesus tells the parable of the rich fool. The man has many positive qualities. He is a hard worker. He is smart. He is financially successful and industrious. And yet he is the only person that Jesus calls a fool. He is a fool because although he knows there is a God, he carries an attitude as if there isn't. He never considers that his life will end. Somehow, he connects many goods with many years, and he makes plans to eat, drink and be merry, live long and luxuriously.

But his life is cut short by the hand of God. The words "This night!" enter into the equation and he is completely unprepared. For although he was rich in this world, he was poor when it came to spiritual matters. No one knows their time! But our time will come, and we are encouraged to keep this in mind.

> *¹³ I also saw under the sun this example of wisdom that greatly impressed me: ¹⁴ There was once a small city with only a few people in it. And a powerful king came against it, surrounded it and built huge siege works against it. ¹⁵ Now there lived in that city a man poor but wise, and he saved the city by his wisdom. But nobody remembered that poor man. ¹⁶ So I said, "Wisdom is better than strength." But the poor man's wisdom is despised, and his words are no longer heeded.*
>
> *¹⁷ The quiet words of the wise are more to be heeded than the shouts of a ruler of fools. ¹⁸ Wisdom is better than weapons of war, but one sinner destroys much good.*

As one would expect, a person's wisdom is something that turns the head of King Solomon. Here he uses the example of wisdom that got his attention.

Often, we forget how powerful wisdom can be. A wise person can change the outcome of so many things as is seen in the King's example.

There is a distinct difference between working hard and working smart. A hard worker will push and push on a large rock to send it down a hill. But a wise person will understand that a long pole placed on top of a small rock can be used as a fulcrum to move the stone easily.

In the example that Solomon gives we see a wise but obscure man delivering the entire city from destruction. It is not clear how he did it. Perhaps he went out and talked to the invading King. Maybe he told him there was nothing in the city worth taking. He may have shared with him a story that turned the ruler's heart. By whatever means, he turned the heart of the leader of the invading army.

In the story *Swiss Family Robinson,* we are introduced to the family as they are on a sinking vessel grabbing all the supplies they could. When they looked up, they saw a pirate ship heading their way. Fighting the pirates was not a viable option. Instead, the father sent a flag up the mast. The flag was a symbol of deadly sickness aboard the ship. Moments later the attacking ship turned around and left. Wisdom won the battle.

Another example of wisdom winning the day took place during the American civil war. General William Tecumseh Sherman was moving from city to city, taking it with ease. When he came to Madison, Georgia, he was met by Senator Joshua Hill. Hill had a friend in Washington D.C. named Senator John Sherman, an Ohio Republican who was Gen. Sherman's brother. The story is told that General Sherman was informed that a woman he had courted years before was living in that city, so he pulled his men back and the city was not burned. One person can indeed make a profound difference!

These are clear examples of the benefits of wisdom. However, although wisdom is honored, the person sharing the wisdom often is left to obscurity. In Solomon's example, the poor man was wise and delivered the city from destruction. But because he was poor, and had no prominence, no one remembered him rescuing the city. Wisdom and wealth often lead to notoriety. Be that as it may, wisdom is still better than strength. Wisdom spoken in quietness can speak louder than a ruler who shouts among fools.

A woman named Marlene had very little education but proved to be wise. Though she was poor she found ways to make life work for her. Because she made good decisions and lived responsibly, she was able to meet all her needs as well as those who depended upon her.

Though Solomon holds wisdom in high regard, he points out that one sinner can do more damage than many weapons.

One of the most destructive weapons people yield is that of the tongue. It is said that the tongue is the first weapon of mass destruction. A Chinese proverb states, "The tongue is a three-inch knife that can kill a six-foot man." Too often the long-time ministry of a pastor has been destroyed by the slandering tongue of one individual. It is little wonder that two of the ten commandments address the tongue.

In James 3:5-10 we read,

> *See how great a forest is set aflame by such a small fire!* [6] *And the tongue is a fire, the very world of iniquity; the tongue is set among our members as that which defiles the entire body, and sets on fire the course of our life, and is set on fire by hell.* [7] *For every species of beasts and birds, of reptiles and creatures of the sea, is tamed and has been tamed by the human race.* [8] *But no one can tame the tongue; it is a restless evil and full of deadly poison.* [9] *With it we bless our Lord and Father, and with it we curse men, who have been made in the likeness of God;* [10] *from the same mouth come both blessing and cursing. My brethren, these things ought not to be this way.*

One sinner, with one loose tongue can bring about great destruction.

King Solomon mentions the destructive abilities of our words when he says, "Death and life are in the power of the tongue." (Proverbs 18:21).

Washington Irving has noted, "A sharp tongue is the only edged tool that grows keener with constant use."

Mary Mallon was a cook in New York City. In 1907 officials from the City Department of Health discovered that she was a carrier of typhoid fever bacteria though she had a resistance to contracting the dreaded disease herself. She became known as "Typhoid Mary."

For three years doctors treated Mary. She signed a commitment not to work as a cook and she reported quarterly to the health Department. Then Mary dropped out of sight.

In 1915 typhoid again erupted among food handlers at a city hospital. The culprit was "Typhoid Mary." Authorities decided the only way to control Mary's infectious influence was to institutionalize her. She was quarantined until her death in 1938.

King Solomon was correct. One sinner can destroy much good!

ECCLESIASTES 10

¹As dead flies give perfume a bad smell, so a little folly outweighs wisdom and honor.

A clear connection can be made from this statement to Ecclesiastes 9:18. It takes a great deal to build something up but very little to tear it down. The old quote "One bad apple spoils the whole barrel" fits well here.

Recently a prominent president of a large university was asked to step down from his position because he was photographed holding a drink while standing with his arm around the waist of a woman who was not his wife. He claimed innocence, but the board of directors saw his folly as harmful to the university and released him.

Folly or foolish behavior can be seen as harmless at the time, but later it can have a profound effect on your life. Over the centuries an old proverb has been handed down illustrating that small things can lead to great results.

> *For Want of a Nail*
> *For want of a nail the shoe was lost.*
> *For want of a shoe the horse was lost.*
> *For want of a horse the rider was lost.*
> *For want of a rider the message was lost.*
> *For want of a message the battle was lost.*
> *For want of a battle the kingdom was lost.*
> *And all for the want of a horseshoe nail.*

One bad comment, one poor decision, one short moment of foolishness can change yours and others' lives. James was correct in pointing out that a very small rudder can steer very large ship! (James 3:4). Likewise, a short stint in folly can change a person's life forever.

> ² *The heart of the wise inclines to the right, but the heart of the fool to the left.*

Moving to the right from a biblical point of view signifies more than just a direction. It demonstrates doing that which is right. The heart of the matter is the matter of the heart! Your heart, your deepest desires will direct your entire life. It will cause you to lean and move in a godly direction.

Recently, a local high school football coach was handed the upcoming opponent's game plan. He looked at the material, recognized it for what it was, and then threw it into the trash adding, "We don't want to win that way." His heart was directing him to make a godly decision.

Conversely, Taylor Smith demonstrated foolishness when she decided to push her sixteen year-old friend off a tall bridge and into the water. When Jordan Holgerson fell, she suffered serious injuries including several broken ribs, a bruise esophagus, an injured trachea, and punctured a lung. Smith's comment was "... I didn't think about the consequences." This is a comment that is consistently heard from those who have foolish hearts.

We are taught early in life that plants will bend and grow toward light. With this in mind, an experiment was done placing a light on one side of a plant and also placing a piece of dark tape on the same side. Over a short period of time, it was found that the plant was growing away from the light. The tape on the stem was blocking the stem's exposure to the light, and it was in fact growing away from the darkness.

And so it is with those who are wise. Their desire is to turn and grow toward the light. But it is with equal importance that they grow away from the dark.

> ³*Even as fools walk along the road, they lack sense*

and show everyone how stupid they are.

Fools are not hard to identify. All one needs to do is follow them. Their foolishness will ooze out eventually. These are not people living a life of adventure, but a life of foolishness.

They will do the following:

- Pet a strange dog or pick up a poisonous snake.
- Step into the road without looking.
- Let a disagreement develop into a physical fight.
- Throw a rock at a passing car.
- Over-indulge in the consumption of alcohol.
- Show off by standing too close to the edge of a cliff.
- Destroy a person's property.

Their behavior will unveil their true selves and observers will see them for the fools they are.

⁴If a ruler's anger rises against you, do not leave your post; calmness can lay great offenses to rest.

The same rules that apply to a tight rope walker can be helpful when dealing with a ruler (or anyone else) who is angry with us. When the wire becomes unsteady for tight rope walkers, they keep four things in mind:

1. Stop! Do not continue! Do not move ahead quickly.
2. Lower your center of gravity.
3. Wait for the wire to stop moving.
4. Move ahead slowly.

If someone in authority comes against us physically or verbally, Solomon's advice is to keep calm no matter what happens.

When conflicts arise several directives should be kept in mind:

- We must maintain our composure and not raise our voice. The anger of your opponent rises with the volume of your voice.

- We must remember that composure changes minds.
- Quite often standing by our convictions can move a ruler's attitude toward us.
- Maintaining our composure often brings admiration.

In Proverbs 15:1, King Solomon stresses the importance of remaining calm during conflict, "A gentle answer turns away wrath, but a harsh word stirs up anger."

This is exemplified in an episode involving a judge and a lawyer. A judge had a pesky lawyer always jawing at him critically. The judge seemed non-plussed by it all. Another attorney asked him about it. "Don't you know and care about all he is saying about you?" The judge wisely replied, "My neighbors have a dog that constantly barks at the moon." Then he paused, and the lawyer asked, "Well, what's the rest of the story?" "Oh," the judge replied, "The moon doesn't say anything. It just goes right on shining!"

Calmness and silence can become your greatest advocate when tensions rise. Abraham Lincoln coined the phrase, "Better to remain silent and be thought a fool than to speak and to remove all doubt."

In Proverbs 17:28, Solomon speaks to this same subject. "Even a fool, when he keeps silent, is considered wise; When he closes his lips, he is *considered* prudent." It is true that when fuel is not added to the fire, the flame dies down.

> *⁵ There is an evil I have seen under the sun, the sort of error that arises from a ruler: ⁶Fools are put in many high positions, while the rich occupy the low ones. ⁷ I have seen slaves on horseback, while princes go on foot like slaves.*

Solomon observed that foolishness and poor judgement can be found everywhere! A person's position is not indicative of their wisdom or ability to lead. There are fools who reside in mansions while wise people live in humble homes.

There is an old saying that too often gets fleshed out in the business world: *People often get promoted to a level of incompetence.*

Sometimes fools can even promote themselves to a higher social status by their foolish acts. However, the fact that they lack sense always seems to be their undoing.

Roger Dillon and Nicole Boyd had financial difficulties. To escape their financial hardship, they decided to rob an armored car. So, on November 26, 2020 they pulled off their heist just north of Youngstown Ohio and made off with $8.4 million. It took very little time for them to be caught and now they face up to 25 years in prison and $250,000 in fines. With the sound of the gavel, they have gone from being independently wealthy to abject poverty and decades of incarceration. Proverbs 21:20 declares, "A fool and his money are soon parted. Dillon and Boyd are living proof of this.

⁸ Whoever digs a pit may fall into it; whoever breaks through a wall may be bitten by a snake. ⁹ Whoever quarries stones may be injured by them; whoever splits logs may be endangered by them.

The King notes that hard work and progress always carry with them the possibility of injury and loss. Life is full of unintended consequences and often brings with it pain. The very area we are trying to move ahead in could be the area where danger lurks. Progress is risky. Be careful to live in the balance between risk and reward and keep a proper perspective. This calls for an approach to life with an equal avoidance between being a muddy-eyed pessimist or a starry-eyed optimist.

In 2018 (the last year statistics are given) it was found that the most dangerous job in America was held by loggers. In that year, 56 loggers died, and 1,040 incurred nonfatal injuries. The most common cause of death was "contact with metal objects and equipment." To make things worse, the median annual wage for this occupation is only $40,650. It is no secret that the logging business is a very difficult trade. Danger lurks behind every log and at the end of every piece of equipment. King Solomon's advice: Be careful! Be very, very careful at whatever you do.

¹⁰ If the ax is dull and its edge unsharpened, more strength is needed, but skill will bring success.

Connecting to the idea of hard work, Solomon embraces the idea of working intelligently. It takes discernment to know whether the lack of intended progress is due to the equipment failure or to the one handling the equipment.

Periodically, there is a need to rest—to *re-tool*. From time to time we need to stop what we're doing and *re-sharpen* our *equipment* and ourselves. We still have the *ax* (the job and the resources of the position), but over time we can lose our sharpness. There are times when we must stop and evaluate our time/progress continuum. If the time we are putting into a job or project is not showing itself in the progress we are making, we must spend some time to *re-sharpen*. This can come in the form of a seminar, class, meeting with other leaders, or just plain rest or disengagement from the task.

When the chain on a chainsaw becomes dull two things happen:

1. The cut through the log becomes curved.

2. We have to apply more pressure (strength) to get through the log. Both of these can lead to injury to the user and damage to the equipment. If we stop and sharpen the saw or replace the chain, the job will be completed with less effort and with more speed and safety.

[11] *If a snake bites before it is charmed, the charmer receives no fee.*

The King cautions us about the problems that are inherent in any business venture. Always enter into any endeavor with proper preparation. *The Five P's of Success* are applicable here: Previous Planning Prevents Poor Performance. Looking ahead while engaged in any task will limit and possibly prevent serious loss. Lack of planning and forethought could cause you to suffer great loss.

A prime example of this took place in 1173 in a town in Italy called Pisa. The town was named by the Greeks in 600 B.C. The word means "Marshy Land." That should have been a clue before construction of the bell tower began. Although the tower is only eight stories high, it carries significant weight which caused the foundation to give way and the tower to lean. After much repair has been done in recent years, the tower still leans between four and five degrees.

King Solomon understood that each opportunity carries with it the idea of timeliness. When our talent is called for, we must not delay and put it off for another day. A delayed response could equal loss. When skills are summoned, run to the task. If a charmer of snakes does not show up and the snake bites, there will be no pay for the owner of the snake or the charmer. Therefore, when opportunity presents itself, expediency is the key.

> *12 Words from the mouth of the wise are gracious, but fools are consumed by their own lips. At the beginning their words are folly; at the end they are wicked madness-and fools multiply words. No one knows what is coming-who can tell someone else what will happen after them? The toil of fools wearies them; they do not know the way to town.*

A comparison between wise people and fools can be seen in the way they talk. Words from wise people are gracious. Words from fools reveal who they are and wind up destroying them.

Solomon indicates that the words from fools have three characteristics:

1. They start as silly statements.
2. They end with craziness.
3. They continue to come with the fools thinking it will eventually make sense to those who are listening.

Regarding his mouth, the fool doesn't seem to understand the old adage regarding holes: When you're in one, stop digging!

Solomon cautions us not to give foolish people an ear. The way they work reveals their lack of common sense. The final commentary on fools is that they don't even have enough sense to work out simple problems such as how to travel to town. We should neither listen to them, nor follow them.

> *16 Woe to the land whose king was a servant and whose princes feast in the morning. Blessed is the land whose king is of noble birth and whose princes eat at*

a proper time—for strength and not for drunkenness.

Good leadership takes wisdom. The land will suffer when under the leadership of someone who is unwise, inexperienced, or untrained. The result will be a leader who celebrates before the day (the work) is complete. This is similar to acting like someone coming out of a successful campaign when they are only going into it.

The land (and the people) are blessed when the leader acts appropriately. He and his team understand the purpose of eating—to equip them for the daily tasks and not simply for enjoyment and drunkenness.

We see the results of foolish decisions in Jesus' parable of the Prodigal Son. He had money, and he had companions. But he did not have the wisdom that brings restraint. Soon, his money and his comrades were gone, and he found himself envying the position of pigs. So it goes with those who have wealth apart from wisdom.

> **[18] Through laziness, the rafters sag; because of idle hands, the house leaks. [19] A feast is made for laughter, wine makes life merry, and money is the answer for everything.**

Solomon is warning us that when we don't pay attention to necessary things, they fall apart, and problems ensue. There are those who lose perspective on their life and lifestyle. They only eat for pleasure and their food selection is made by their tongue and not their brain. Wine is used by them to cover up the seriousness of problems (like sagging rafters and a leaky house), in life and they believe that money solves all their problems.

In Matthew 25:1-13, Jesus spoke about being on the alert for the coming of the kingdom. Although He was speaking on a spiritual level, the apex of the story has to do with diligence and readiness.

Then the kingdom of heaven will be comparable to ten virgins, who took their lamps and went out to meet the bridegroom.

> *[2] Five of them were foolish, and five were prudent. [3] For when the foolish took their lamps, they took no oil with them, [4] but the prudent took oil in flasks along with*

their lamps. ⁵ Now while the bridegroom was delaying, they all got drowsy and began to sleep. ⁶ But at midnight there was a shout, 'Behold, the bridegroom! Come out to meet him.' ⁷ Then all those virgins rose and trimmed their lamps. ⁸ The foolish said to the prudent, 'Give us some of your oil, for our lamps are going out.' ⁹ But the prudent answered, 'No, there will not be enough for us and you too; go instead to the dealers and buy some for yourselves.' ¹⁰ And while they were going away to make the purchase, the bridegroom came, and those who were ready went in with him to the wedding feast; and the door was shut. ¹¹ Later the other virgins also came, saying, 'Lord, lord, open up for us.' ¹² But he answered, 'Truly I say to you, I do not know you.' ¹³ Be on the alert then, for you do not know the day nor the hour.

Whether we are addressing spiritual issues or physical issues, there is a loud call for the proper perspective. Neglect brings difficulties and sometimes disaster.

²⁰ Do not revile the king even in your thoughts, or curse the rich in your bedroom, because a bird in the sky may carry your words, and a bird on the wing will make the matter known.

King Solomon let's us know that the walls have ears! We are encouraged to be very careful what we say and to whom we say it both publicly and privately. Many times those matters get carried to the public's attention and the results could be very problematic.

Solomon's warning is to not even think thoughts against others lest your thoughts become words and lead to your undoing. Jesus said in Matthew 12:34, "...out of the abundance of the heart the mouth speaks."

Today, the internet grabs and holds your comments and pictures for all time and you fall into the interpretation and judgment of those who see it.

This was seen in the life of a college student thirty years ago. She had too much to drink and lifted her shirt exposing herself. Someone took a picture and circulated it. Although that was thirty years ago, and she was under the influence of alcohol, her past actions are viewed under present eyes. This resulted in her reputation being tarnished and her being required to step down from her position of teaching Sunday school to middle schoolers in her church.

For over 20 years, Jerry Richardson had been the majority owner of the Carolina Panthers. The Panthers experienced great success including six division titles and two appearances in the Super Bowl. But in 2018, he was forced to sell the team due to misconduct in the workplace involving sexually suggestive language and behavior, and on at least one occasion directing a racial slur at an African-American Panther's scout.

You may not notice who is around (a bird) and you may not realize that they carry your words to others. It is not possible to un-blow a trumpet. The best course is not to think and certainly not to voice critical opinions of those around you.

Next, we find Solomon's advice in several areas. In just ten verses, he addresses finances, diligence, and the proper perspective on life in general.

ECCLESIASTES 11

¹Ship your grain across the sea; after many days you may receive a return. ² Invest in seven ventures, yes, in eight; you do not know what disaster may come upon the land. ³ If clouds are full of water, they pour rain on the earth. Whether a tree falls to the south or to the north, in the place where it falls, there it will lie.

FINANCE

Solomon advises us to diversify our investment portfolio. We are to spread our wealth among many different ventures. When one does not do well, the others will pick up the loss. In the stock market this is called "dollar averaging." It is done by investing a set amount of money each month. When the stocks are high you buy less shares, but each share is worth more. When the stocks are down, you are able to buy more shares at a lower price.

Solomon's next piece of advice regarding finances involves patience. Be patient! It takes time for investments to mature. Do not be impatient or impulsive, but let the process run its course. When a cloud is full of water, it brings a return of water. When wise investments are made a return can be expected. When a tree falls and lies on the ground it decays over time and gives back to the earth. All of this takes time and we must be willing to let our investments run their course.

⁴ Whoever watches the wind will not plant; whoever looks at the clouds will not reap. ⁵ As you do not know the path of the wind, or how the body is formed in a mother's womb, so you cannot understand the work of God, the Maker of all things. ⁶ Sow your seed in the morning, and at evening let your hands not be idle, for you do not know which will succeed, whether this or that, or whether both will do equally well.

DILIGENCE

Many people suffer from what has been called, "The paralysis of analysis." If a farmer fails to plant for fear his seed will blow away or wash away, harvest time will yield nothing.

There are those who make excuses (some of them ridiculous) for their lack of diligence. The King addresses this in Proverbs 22:13, "The sluggard says, 'There is a lion outside; I will be killed in the streets!'"

Nothing gets done by merely thinking about it, but nothing gets done well without the energy of thought. Climbing a tree yields a better view than sitting on an acorn and waiting for it to grow. The mountain does *not* get smaller by staring at it and progress is not made by wishing for it. You do not know the best time to put effort into your work so commit to working consistently with excellence.

In the Middle 17th century a judge in Hanford, Ct. was presiding when an eclipse of the sun occurred. The courtroom began to panic. Whereupon the judge rapped the gavel for order and said: "If this be the end of the world, let us at least be found doing our duty. Bring in the candles!"

Difficulty is the enemy of diligence and it is an adversary that anyone who is pursuing success will meet. The call to persistence in the face of adversity is worded clearly by Ted Engstrom:

> *Cripple him, and you have a Sir Walter Scott. Lock him in a prison cell, and you have a John Bunyan. Bury him in the snows of Valley Forge, and you have a George Washington. Raise him in abject poverty and you have an Abraham Lincoln. Strike him down with infantile paralysis, and he becomes Franklin Roosevelt. Burn him so severely that doctors say he'll never walk again, and you have a Glenn Cunningham - who set the world's one-*

mile record in 1934. Deafen him and you have a Ludwig van Beethoven. Have him or her born black in a society filled with racial discrimination, and you have a Booker T. Washington, a Marian Anderson, a George Washington Carver... Call him a slow learner, "retarded," and write him off as uneducable, and you have an Albert Einstein.

Difficult times are not necessarily your enemy. As Michael Hopf notes: "Hard times create strong men, strong men create good times, good times create weak men, and weak men create hard times."

PERSPECTIVE ON LIFE

⁷ Light is sweet, and it pleases the eyes to see the sun. ⁸ However many years anyone may live, let them enjoy them all. But let them remember the days of darkness, for there will be many. Everything to come is meaningless.

Solomon urges us to enjoy our days that are good and reflect on the days of struggle. Remembering the bad days draws you to be thankful for the good days. It heightens your enjoyment of them. The good days become sweeter when placed next to the bad days.

- An hour in the cold makes you appreciate the heat.
- Missing a meal helps you enjoy your next one.
- Sleeping on the ground brings appreciation for a bed.
- Great thirst sets one up to relish a cold drink.
- A day filled with loneliness brings fulfillment in the presence of friends.

Solomon continues his admonition on life and focuses on those who have youth on their side.

⁹ You who are young, be happy while you are young, and let your heart give you joy in the days of your youth. Follow the ways of your heart and whatev-

er your eyes see, but know that for all these things God will bring you into judgment. ¹⁰ So then, banish anxiety from your heart and cast off the troubles of your body, for youth and vigor are meaningless.

King Solomon understood that childhood is a time full of energy and excitement. His encouragement is for us to follow our dreams! Explore! Invest! Experience! But with all that activity, it is important to measure our activity and choices against the knowledge that someday God WILL judge us for our choices and activities. He IS the final judge! Life is brief (meaningless) and will at some point come to an end. This is a call for balance in activity and pursuits.

Henry Wadsworth Longfellow (1807-1882) penned these words in "A Psalm of Life:

WHAT THE HEART OF THE YOUNG MAN
SAID TO THE PSALMIST;

Tell me not, in mournful numbers,
Life is but an empty dream! —
For the soul is dead that slumbers,
And things are not what they seem.
Life is real! Life is earnest!
And the grave is not its goal;
Dust thou art, to dust returnest,
Was not spoken of the soul.
Not enjoyment, and not sorrow,
Is our destined end or way;
But to act, that each to-morrow
Find us farther than to-day.
Art is long, and time is fleeting,
And our hearts, though stout and brave,
Still, like muffled drums, are beating
Funeral marches to the grave.
In the world's broad field of battle,
In the bivouac of life,
Be not like dumb, driven cattle!
Be a hero in the strife!

Trust no future, howe'er pleasant!
Let the dead past bury its dead!
Act,— act in the living present!
Heart within, and God o'erhead!
Lives of great men all remind us
We can make our lives sublime,
And, departing, leave behind us
Footprints on the sands of time;
Footprints, that perhaps another,
Sailing o'er life's solemn main,
A forlorn and shipwrecked brother,
Seeing, shall take heart again.
Let us, then, be up and doing,
With a heart for any fate;
Still achieving, still pursuing,
Learn to labor and to wait.

This is a poem that runs parallel to what Solomon is proclaiming. Give life all you've got, but keep your heart within you and God over your head.

ECCLESIASTES 12

¹Remember your Creator in the days of your youth, before the days of trouble come and the years approach when you will say, "I find no pleasure in them" ² before the sun and the light and the moon and the stars grow dark, and the clouds return after the rain; ³ when the keepers of the house tremble, and the strong men stoop, when the grinders cease because they are few, and those looking through the windows grow dim; ⁴ when the doors to the street are closed and the sound of grinding fades; when people rise up at the sound of birds, but all their songs grow faint; ⁵when people are afraid of heights and of dangers in the streets; when the almond tree blossoms and the grasshopper drags itself along and desire no longer is stirred. Then people go to their eternal home mourners go about the street. ⁶ Remember him—before the silver cord is severed, and the golden bowl is broken; before the pitcher is shattered at the spring, and the wheel broken at the well, ⁷ and the dust returns to the ground it came from, and the spirit returns to God who gave it. ⁸ "Meaningless! Meaningless!" says the Teacher. "Everything is meaningless!"

Following is the longest continual train of thought that Solomon penned. He is centered on the aging process and the importance of remembering God during the days of youthfulness, before it is too late and the ability to process things clearly escapes.

THE AGING PROCESS

Solomon uses a series of metaphors regarding growing old. He cautions those who are young to never leave God out of the equation. The youthful days will pass-but God will not! He stresses keeping Him in mind as one goes throughout his youthful days. The joys, opportunities, excitement, and energy of being young will pass leaving in their place a body that has aged and is not able to do what was once done.

In Mark 14:38 Jesus is speaking regarding temptation when He says, "Keep watching and praying that you may not come into temptation; the spirit is willing, but the flesh is weak."

Although Jesus is specifically speaking about temptation and the importance of keeping alert to resist it, this can equally be applied to the topic Solomon is addressing. Our minds think of so many things that our bodies have lost the ability to perform. Many people get hurt physically because they misjudge what their bodies can do. Their minds have not kept pace with their aging bodies, and they cannot perform the tasks their minds assign themselves.

Nature moves on and what used to be done in the day and night will not be done any more.

Following are the series of metaphors the King is using. Some are more obvious than others:

The watchmen - The purpose of the watchmen is for protection. In terms of the human body, protection is achieved by use of your arms and hands. The arms are used to shield the body and the hands are used to grasp objects to prevent a fall. However, as time goes on, the arms and hands have a tendency to tremble and shake.

The mighty men - The strongest muscles in the human body are the combined muscles of the legs. Over time, because of inflammation, loss of strength, and other ailments, a person's legs will tend to lose their ability to strengthen and a person will stoop.

The grinding ones - Obviously he is speaking here of the teeth. Tooth decay,tooth loss, and gum issues will cause these grinding ones to be limited in their use. Steak and potatoes will eventually be replaced by pre-blended recipes.

The windows - Even while wearing glasses (windows) the ability of the eyes diminishes.

The doors to the street - What lets us know what is going on outside in the street are our ears. As we age our ability to hear common sounds (such as a mill) is greatly hindered.

The elderly have a tendency to rise early (with the birds) yet their ability to enjoy the songs of the birds is truncated.

The fear of heights and danger creeps in - Personal safety becomes a priority. A fall for an elderly person is much more serious than that of a young person. Healing doesn't come as quickly for them and fear becomes a stronger part of their outlook. An aging person can look at a ladder and conclude, "I might fall." A young person may look at the same ladder and conclude, "I might not fall."

Fear of danger from strangers in the street can also become part of the aging person's mind-set. The elderly lose their ability to defend themselves against physical attacks and may feel extremely vulerable.

The almond tree - The blossoms of an almond tree are white. This signifies the aging process turning a person's hair white or grey.

The grasshopper - Solomon is aluding to sexual desire. Sexual interest wanes and a person is no longer stirred by the prospects of physical intimacy.

At some point, death comes taking a person's body. Mourners come and pay their respects, but in the end, they go on with their business and lives. The person's life ends, but the lives of those who knew the deceased continues on in the usual way.

Again, King Solomon stresses the importance of having a God-centered mind-set. The time to think about God is when you are young, before the mind goes and reason fails.

In Proverbs 10:27 Solomon instructs us, *The fear of the Lord prolongs life, but the years of the wicked will be shortened.*

To fear the Lord is to hold Him in reverence and honor. Recently this bit of biblical wisdom has been discovered anew by medical science.

A new study by Duke University shows that older people who have an active faith may be healthier than those who don't. Researchers studied 4000 North Carolinians over age 65 and found that those who participated in religious activities (fearing the Lord) were 40% less likely to have high blood pressure which is a warning sign for heart disease. The study reported in a recent issue of the International Journal of psychiatric medicine found that after adjusting for differences in gender, race, age, and other factors there was still a significant difference in diastolic blood pressure readings for those who attended weekly religious services, those who read the Bible regularly, and those who prayed regularly. Researchers suggested that religious faith (the fear of the Lord) may serve as a source of comfort for older people lowering stress in their lives.

The silver cord is life itself. Life will come to an end for all of us and this cord will be broken.

The golden bowl stands for our memory and mental abilities which wane over time.

Solomon next couples two metaphors together each signifying difficulties to come.

The pitcher is our ability to learn and take in information. The wheel at the Cistern stands for our ability to engage/reason/debate.

When going to a cistern to gather water, there are two inherent needs: Something in which to carry the water (a pitcher), and a means to gather the water from the cistern (the wheel).

Conversations, ideas, and information along with our ability to gather them are gained and carried much more easily when we are young. But as we age, we forget more and our ability to learn decreases.

The end will come, and God will re-claim a man's soul and he will stand before the one who made him. A person's body will be enveloped by the ground and decay, but his spirit will go to God before whom he will stand.

In Romans 14:10, the Apostle Paul addresses the idea of God's judgment when he says, "But you, why do you judge your brother? Or you again, why do you regard your brother with contempt? For we will all stand before the judgment seat of God."

In Hebrews 4:13, the writer also addresses the idea of God's judgment, "And there is no creature hidden from His sight, but all things are open and laid bare to the eyes of Him with whom we have to do.

Our bodies may go down to the earth, but our souls will ascend to God for His righteous judgment. Solomon is telling us in clear terms that as we live our life, we must be mindful of the end of our life and the judgment to come.

He closes out this section with his continual reminder that life is brief and all of life fades. God and God alone remains.

Our lives are full of examples of those who have the physical attributes that Solomon has described in the aging process but have also kept their focus on God. One such example comes to us in the life of Charlie. When Charlie was young, he grabbed life by the horns. He went to school, played sports, and led a highly active social life. With an outgoing personality he was the life of the party and people were naturally drawn to him. After college, he taught and coached football and track and used his position to influence the lives of countless young people.

Charlie would often share a quote from Thomas Friedman that demonstrated his attitude toward life:

> *Every morning in Africa, a gazelle wakes up. It knows it must run faster than the fastest lion, or it will be killed. Every morning a lion wakes up. It knows it must outrun the slowest gazelle, or it will starve to death. It doesn't matter whether you are a lion or a gazelle, when the sun comes up, you better start running.*

But in all his doing, Charlie kept his relationship with the Lord on center stage. He read his Bible, prayed, led a student ministry, and served in his church. He had an active faith and used it to lead his friends and family. He remembered the Lord in all he did and served him *before the silver cord was severed, and the golden bowl was broken; before the pitcher was shattered at the spring, and the wheel broken at the well.*

And because he kept God on the front burner of his life, when Charlie's spirit went up to God, he could stand unashamed.

The script writers alluded to this idea in the movie, *Rudy*. Rudy is desperate to get into the University of Notre Dame to play football for the Fighting Irish. In a last ditch effort to get in, he finds himself in a Catholic church near campus. An elderly priest sees him and engages him in conversation. Rudy explains his desire and essentially asks if the priest could put in a good word for him with God. The priest explains, "Son, in thirty-five years of religious studies, I've come up with only two hard, incontrovertible facts: There is a God... and I'm not Him."

In the following section, it is possible that Solomon allowed his writer to interject his own thoughts on all that the King had dictated. It is equally possible that Solomon stepped into the third-party voice to share his purpose in all that he had previously verbalized. Whether his copiest weighed in on it or he said it, it is undeniable that Solomon felt this way.

> *⁹ Not only was the Teacher wise, but he also imparted knowledge to the people. He pondered and searched out and set in order many proverbs. ¹⁰ The Teacher searched to find just the right words, and what he wrote was upright and true.*

King Solomon was admitedly and obviously wise. But beyond possessing wisdom, he sought to share that wisdom with the people under his charge. He desired to share with them that which he held to be both upright and true.

We all need direction! Everyone is in a position to teach something to someone. Thomas Carlyle notes, "Every man is my superior in that I may learn from him."

It is not enough to have knowledge-you must do something with the knowledge you have which is by definition, wisdom.

It is noted that Solomon desired to teach truth through the use of a multitude of proverbs. In fact, most of the words penned in the book of proverbs, come from the mind of King Solomon. A proverb is a truth presented in a way that is easy to understand, remember, and apply.

He desired both to find pleasant words to share and share truth in a correct manner.

Truth is in fact independent of feelings, opinions, or desires.

Today we find more and more people desiring "personal truth."

They claim there are no absolute truths. They say, "Anyone who believes in absolutes is a fool," but that claim is an absolute. In fact, all truth is absolute. That is, it is true for all people in all places at all times. An example of this would be seen in the statement: "On Tuesday I went to the dentist." If I went to the dentist on Tuesday, that fact is true for all people, in all places for all time. It is an absolute fact.

Along with this, it needs to be noted that a basic law of logic states that two opposing statements cannot both be true in the same way, at the same time. This is known as *the law of non-contradiction*.

So the claim that *what he wrote was upright and true* must pass through the grid of truth as well as the law of non-contradiction. King Solomon would make the claim that his words do in fact, pass both of these requirements and should therefore be accepted.

> *¹¹ The words of the wise are like goads, their collected sayings like firmly embedded nails-given by one shepherd. ¹² Be warned, my son, of anything in addition to them.*

Goads are sticks or rods with points on the end used to cause animals to move in a particular direction. They are not used to inflict harm or to destroy the animal. The goal of a goad is to inflict a little discomfort to cause the animal to go the right way.

Similarly, words of wise men bring direction. They move us away from danger and in a good direction. The goal is to master these words of wisdom and let them sink deep into our hearts like a nail driven into wood. These words bring security and hold us fast. They fasten us to the place where we belong.

When metal is driven into a tree, over time, it will leave a faint blue mark running up and down on the inside of the tree. Tree cutters who see this blue mark are careful to look for metal inside the tree in order to avoid damaging their saws. Just as metal has an impact on a tree and affects the wood, wisdom has an impact on a person and affects their life.

King Solomon admonishes his son (and us) not to follow the words of those who are not wise. These include words that are added to the words of the wise. In Proverbs 1:8-19, The King warns his son regarding following the wrong (unwise) crowd:

> *⁸Hear, my son, your father's instruction*
> *And do not forsake your mother's teaching;*

⁹ Indeed, they are a graceful wreath to your head
And ornaments about your neck.
¹⁰ My son, if sinners entice you,
Do not consent.
¹¹ If they say, "Come with us,
Let us lie in wait for blood,
Let us ambush the innocent without cause;
¹² Let us swallow them alive like Sheol,
Even whole, as those who go down to the pit;
¹³ We will find all kinds of precious wealth,
We will fill our houses with spoil;
¹⁴ Throw in your lot with us,
We shall all have one purse,"
¹⁵ My son, do not walk in the way with them.
Keep your feet from their path,
¹⁶ For their feet run to evil
And they hasten to shed blood.
¹⁷ Indeed, it is useless to spread the baited net
In the sight of any bird;
¹⁸ But they lie in wait for their own blood;
They ambush their own lives.
¹⁹ So are the ways of everyone who gains by violence;
It takes away the life of its possessors.

King Solomon understood the enticement of inclusion and tells his son to avoid those who would include him in their wrong ways. In short, he makes the claim that they don't even have the wisdom of birds. Perhaps this is the first time the phrase "bird brain" is suggested.

Of making many books there is no end, and much study wearies the body.

Solomon showed particular insight by the above statement. We see the reality of the endless writing of books in our day. The U.S. Library of Congress houses more than 32 million catalogued books and other print materials in 470 languages; In 2018 alone, the office had registered over 38 million claims to works of authorship.

And for works published after 1977, the copyright lasts for the life of the author plus 70 years. But not all books that are copyrighted are true and not all of them will lead us down the path of wisdom. A further reason to be careful about what we listen to and who we follow.

If one is mindful of them, one can quickly notice the "Goads" in their lives. These are words that give direction, information, encouragement, and warning.

Dear reader, please allow me to digress to a personal note. My life (and I'm certain yours) has been full of "Goads." They have come from parents, friends, employers, coaches, teachers, and siblings. They have become a source of wisdom and have guided me in my personal journey of life.

Most of the people who gave me guidance did so by the way they lived but many also shared words that I've never forgotten. These people walked beside me or in front of me.

THE "GOADS" IN MY LIFE
Dad:
"If you lie down with dogs, you wake up with fleas."
"There are times when you are dead right, but you are still dead.
"Doing it right beats doing it over."
"The impossible is possible if you aren't aware it's impossible."
"Sometimes, genius and insanity are closely related."
"Today it's me. Tomorrow, it's you!"

Mom:
"People are like houses. They can look good on the outside but be empty on the inside."
"He who fights and runs away, lives to fight another day."
"Even though you only see clouds, the sun is still shining."

Mr. Brown:
"You can get into more trouble in five minutes than you can work your way out of in a lifetime."

Rev. Stephen Crotts:
"The best revenge is living well."
"If you treat your wife like a queen, you get to be the king."
"A Healthy Church:

Hands down the Word
Reaches up in worship
Reaches inward in pastoral care
Reaches out in missions locally and abroad
It remembers its past in heritage with pride,
but also embraces its future and change in growth and the new things that God is doing."

Gareth "Lefty" Biser:
"Remember the 5 p's: Previous Planning Prevents Poor Performance."
"You can spend a dollar any way you want, but you can only spend it once."
"You can if you have to.
"It is possible to be a victim of 'Self-tacklization.'"
"You cannot surprise God."

Coach Tom Doherty:
"Don't tell me, show me."
"Hard work always pays off!"
"The only thing left to do is to do it."

Steve Wilt:
"Always leave things better than you found them."

Perry Tuttle:
"God always has more than enough to meet your needs."

Ronnie Deal:
"There's a right way, and a wrong way to leave any job."

General Dick Abel:
"Your heart is only broken because God has someone better planned."
"God gives the best to those who leave the choice to Him."
"You serve those whom you lead."

Bob Long:
"Always cut the wood in front of you."

Walt Wiley:
"Encouragement is food for the soul."

Coach Pete Dyer:
"Talk is cheap except on the telephone."
"If they don't score, we don't lose."

Ralph Henderson:
"Father time is undefeated."

Colin Pinkney:
"Be careful not to judge people-You don't know their story."

Tony Pierce:
"No matter how things look, God is still in control."

Terry Johnson:
"God promises no help for noncommissioned work."

Kay Yow:
"All it takes is all you've got."

Reverend Chris Justice:
"'Can't' died in the battle of 'Try.'"

> *13 **The conclusion, when all has been heard, is: fear God and keep His commandments, because this applies to every person. 14 For God will bring every act to judgment, everything which is hidden, whether it is good or evil.***

Here we come, after a long and deep voyage with King Solomon, to his final conclusion! This is a point of total application: For all men and all women for all time in every place. There are no exceptions!

1. Honor God (fear Him) with your life. Carry a deep reverence for him reflected in an understanding of who He is and His power and majesty just as you would a majestic and powerful king.

2. Obey the commands of God.

In John 14:15 Jesus said, "If you love Me, you will keep My commandments." Those who love, obey. With God, we don't obey in order to cause Him to love us. We obey because we know He loves us!

These two commands go hand in hand and cannot be separated from one another. We cannot honor God without obeying His commands. Likewise, we will not obey God unless we have a reverence for Him.

In the end, nothing (no deed and no person) is hidden from God. He WILL bring it all (good and bad) into His judgment.

CONCLUSION

This tour with a man endowed with wisdom from God has taken us through subjects such as: The value of wisdom, interpersonal relationships, honoring God and others, living a balanced life, keeping a proper perspective, the brevity of life and a host of other topics.

King Solomon's goal was to impart wisdom so that those who would follow his advice would find not only a better life, but a fulfilling after-life.

The old adage is true, "A word to the wise is sufficient." And regarding the reading of the words from the teacher, a word from the wise is life changing and fulfilling!

It's been said that, "Impression without expression, leads to stagnation." We been seated for a very long time at the feet of one endowed with wisdom from the heavenly Father.

There are two key aspects to any set of information. They are the "What?" and the "So What?" King Solomon has given us a plethora of "What?" It now falls to each of us to develop the "So what?" for the application of all that he has shared. Understanding this leads us to the natural question, now that you know, how will you go?

Without question, the information we have covered from the mind of Solomon will hold each of us in good stead if we will but apply it to our lives.

ABOUT THE AUTHOR
DR. STEVEN A. JIRGAL

Dr. Jirgal is a 1980 graduate of Gettysburg College where he became a four-time conference champion, All-American, and inductee to the Middle Atlantic Conferecnce *All Century Team* in the pole vault. He holds an undergraduate degree in health education and physical education. Following graduation, he taught on the high school and college level while coaching football and track in both venues. He holds masters degrees in health education, sports medicine, and divinity, as well as a doctorate in ministry.

He has been the director of Sports Medicine at Wingate University, area director for the Fellowship of Christian Athletes and has served on the staff of Hickory Grove Baptist Church in Charlotte, NC, as well as leading Lakeview Baptist Church, in Monroe, NC and Anderson Grove Baptist Church as the Senior Pastor. He presently serves as the "Pastor to the Pastors" at Lee Park Church. He has served on the local board of directors for the Fellowship of Christian Athletes, the board of trustees at New Orleans Baptist Seminary and the ministerial board of Wingate University. He currently serves on the board of directors for The Carolina Study Center, and Fathers in Touch ministry.

Dr. Jirgal is the founder and director of *The Jirgal Leadership Institute* where he strives to equip people for success in leadership roles. He and his wife Pam have three children, Joshua, Caleb, and Sarah. They reside in Monroe, NC.

OTHER BOOKS BY DR. JIRGAL
(DESCRIPTIONS TO BE FOUND ON THE JIRGAL
LEADERSHIP WEBSITE AT JIRGALLEADERSHIP.COM)

The Path of a Champion
Dying to Live
Life Points
Laws to Live By
Principles of Wholeness
Running a Clean Race
Encounters with the Christ
The Going to Bed Book
Intentional Steps
52 Words
Mining the Mind of King Solomon

www.ingramcontent.com/pod-product-compliance
Lightning Source LLC
Chambersburg PA
CBHW060649150426
42813CB00052B/503